The Ultimate ENGAA Guide

UniAdmissions

ISBN 978-0-9935711-6-9

Published by *RAR Medical Services Limited*
www.uniadmissions.co.uk
info@uniadmissions.co.uk
Tel: 0208 068 0438

The Ultimate ENGAA Guide

250 Practice Questions

Dr Rohan Agarwal

About the Author

Rohan is the **Director of Operations** at *UniAdmissions* and is responsible for its technical and commercial arms. He graduated from Gonville and Caius College, Cambridge and is a fully qualified doctor. Over the last five years, he has tutored hundreds of successful Oxbridge and Medical applicants. He has also authored ten books on admissions tests and interviews.

Rohan has taught physiology to undergraduates and interviewed medical school applicants for Cambridge. He has published research on bone physiology and writes education articles for the Independent and Huffington Post. In his spare time, Rohan enjoys playing the piano and table tennis.

The Basics

What is the ENGAA?

The Engineering Admissions Assessment (ENGAA) is a two-hour written exam taken by prospective Cambridge Engineering applicants.

What does the ENGAA consist of?

Section	Timing	SKILLS TESTED	Questions	Caclulator
ONE	80 Minutes	1A: Maths and Physics 1B: Advanced Maths & Physics	28 MCQs 26 MCQs	Not Allowed
TWO	40 Minutes	Advanced Maths and Advanced Physics	17 MCQs	Allowed

Why is the ENGAA used?

Cambridge Engineering applicants tend to be a bright bunch and therefore usually have excellent grades with many having over 90% in all of their A level subjects. This means that competition is fierce – meaning that the universities must use the ENGAA to help differentiate between applicants.

When do I sit ENGAA?

The ENGAA takes place in the first week of November every year, normally on a Wednesday Morning.

Can I resit the ENGAA?

No, you can only sit the ENGAA once per admissions cycle.

Where do I sit the ENGAA?

You can usually sit the ENGAA at your school or college (ask your exams officer for more information). Alternatively, if your school isn't a registered test centre or you're not attending a school or college, you can sit the ENGAA at an authorised test centre.

Do I have to resit the ENGAA if I reapply?
Yes - you cannot use your score from any previous attempts.

How is the ENGAA Scored?
In section 1, each question carries one mark and there is no negative marking. In section 2, marks for each question are indicated alongside it. Unless stated otherwise, you will only score marks for correct answers if you show your working.

How is the ENGAA used?
Different Cambridge colleges will place different weightings on different components so its important you find out as much information about how your marks will be used by emailing the college admissions office.

In general, the university will interview a high proportion of realitstic applicants so the ENGAA score isn't vital for making the interview shortlist. However, it can play a huge role in the final decision after your interview

General Advice

Start Early

It is much easier to prepare if you practice little and often. Start your preparation well in advance; ideally by mid September but at the latest by early October. This way you will have plenty of time to complete as many papers as you wish to feel comfortable and won't have to panic and cram just before the test, which is a much less effective and more stressful way to learn. In general, an early start will give you the opportunity to identify the complex issues and work at your own pace.

Prioritise

Some questions in the ENGAA can be long and complex – and given the intense time pressure you need to know your limits. It is essential that you don't get stuck with very difficult questions. If a question looks particularly long or complex, mark it for review and move on. You don't want to be caught 5 questions short at the end just because you took more than 3 minutes in answering a challenging multi-step physics question. If a question is taking too long, choose a sensible answer and move on. Remember that each question carries equal weighting and therefore, you should adjust your timing in accordingly. With practice and discipline, you can get very good at this and learn to maximise your efficiency.

Positive Marking

There are no penalties for incorrect answers in the ENGAA; you will gain one for each right answer and will not get one for each wrong or unanswered one. This provides you with the luxury that you can always guess should you absolutely be not able to figure out the right answer for a question or run behind time. Since each question provides you with 4 to 6 possible answers, you have a 16-25% chance of guessing correctly. Therefore, if you aren't sure (and are running short of time), then make an educated guess and move on.

Before 'guessing' you should try to eliminate a couple of answers to increase your chances of getting the question correct. For example, if a question has 5 options and you manage to eliminate 2 options- your chances of getting the question increase from 20% to 33%!

Avoid losing easy marks on other questions because of poor exam technique. Similarly, if you have failed to finish the exam, take the last 10 seconds to guess the remaining questions to at least give yourself a chance of getting them right.

Practice

This is the best way of familiarising yourself with the style of questions and the timing for this section. You are unlikely to be familiar with the style of questions when you first encounter them. Therefore, you want to be comfortable at using this before you sit the test.

Practising questions will put you at ease and make you more comfortable with the exam. The more comfortable you are, the less you will panic on the test day and the more likely you are to score highly. Initially, work through the questions at your own pace, and spend time carefully reading the questions and looking at any additional data. When it becomes closer to the test, **make sure you practice the questions under exam conditions**.

Past Papers

The ENGAA is a very new exam so there aren't many past papers available. Specimen papers are freely available online at **www.uniadmissions.co.uk/ENGAA**. Once you've worked your way through the questions in this book, you are highly advised to attempt them.

Repeat Questions

When checking through answers, pay particular attention to questions you have got wrong. If there is a worked answer, look through that carefully until you feel confident that you understand the reasoning, and then repeat the question without help to check that you can do it. If only the answer is given, have another look at the question and try to work out why that answer is correct. This is the best way to learn from your mistakes, and means you are less likely to make similar mistakes when it comes to the test.

The same applies for questions which you were unsure of and made an educated guess which was correct, even if you got it right. When working through this book, **make sure you highlight any questions you are unsure of**, this means you know to spend more time looking over them once marked.

Calculators

You are only permitted to use calculators in section 2 – thus, it is essential that you have strong numerical skills. For instance, you should be able to rapidly convert between percentages, decimals and fractions. You will seldom get questions that would require calculators but you would be expected to be able to arrive at a sensible estimate. Consider for example:

Estimate 3.962 x 2.322:

3.962 is approximately 4 and 2.323 is approximately 2.33 = 7/3.

Thus, $3.962 \times 2.322 \approx 4 \times \frac{7}{3} = \frac{28}{3} = 9.33$

Since you will rarely be asked to perform difficult calculations, you can use this as a signpost of if you are tackling a question correctly. For example, when solving a physics question in section 1, you end up having to divide 8,079 by 357- this should raise alarm bells as calculations in the ENGAA are rarely this difficult.

A word on timing...

"If you had all day to do your ENGAA, you would get 100%. But you don't."

Whilst this isn't completely true, it illustrates a very important point. Once you've practiced and know how to answer the questions, the clock is your biggest enemy. This seemingly obvious statement has one very important consequence. **The way to improve your ENGAA score is to improve your speed.** There is no magic bullet. But there are a great number of techniques that, with practice, will give you significant time gains, allowing you to answer more questions and score more marks.

Timing is tight throughout the ENGAA – **mastering timing is the first key to success.** Some candidates choose to work as quickly as possible to save up time at the end to check back, but this is generally not the best way to do it. ENGAA questions can have a lot of information in them – each time you start answering a question it takes time to get familiar with the instructions and information. By splitting the question into two sessions (the first run-through and the return-to-check) you double the amount of time you spend on familiarising yourself with the data, as you have to do it twice instead of only once. This costs valuable time.

In addition, candidates who do check back may spend 2–3 minutes doing so and yet not make any actual changes. Whilst this can be reassuring, it is a false reassurance as it is unlikely to have a significant effect on your actual score. Therefore it is usually best to pace yourself very steadily, aiming to spend the same amount of time on each question and finish the final question in a section just as time runs out. This reduces the time spent on re-familiarising with questions and maximises the time spent on the first attempt, gaining more marks.

It is essential that you don't get stuck with the hardest questions – no doubt there will be some. In the time spent answering only one of these you may miss out on answering three easier questions. If a question is taking too long, choose a sensible answer and move on. Never see this as giving up or in any way failing, rather it is the smart way to approach a test with a tight time limit.

With practice and discipline, you can get very good at this and learn to maximise your efficiency. It is not about being a hero and aiming for full marks – this is almost impossible and very much unnecessary (even Oxbridge will regard any score higher than 7 as exceptional). It is about maximising your efficiency and gaining the maximum possible number of marks within the time you have.

Top tip! Ensure that you take a watch that can show you the time in seconds into the exam. This will allow you have a much more accurate idea of the time you're spending on a question. In general, if you've spent >120 seconds on a section 1 question - move on regardless of how close you think you are to solving it.

Use the Options:

Some questions may try to overload you with information. When presented with large tables and data, it's essential you look at the answer options so you can focus your mind. This can allow you to reach the correct answer a lot more quickly. Consider the example below:

The table below shows the results of a study investigating antibiotic resistance in staphylococcus populations. A single staphylococcus bacterium is chosen at random from a similar population. Resistance to any one antibiotic is independent of resistance to others.

Antibiotic	Number of Bacteria tested	Number of Resistant Bacteria
Benzyl-penicillin	10^{11}	98
Chloramphenicol	10^9	1200
Metronidazole	10^8	256
Erythromycin	10^5	2

Calculate the probability that the bacterium selected will be resistant to all four drugs.

A   1 in 10^6 C   1 in 10^{20} E   1 in 10^{30}

B   1 in 10^{12} D   1 in 10^{25} F   1 in 10^{35}

Looking at the options first makes it obvious that there is **no need to calculate exact values**- only in powers of 10. This makes your life a lot easier. If you hadn't noticed this, you might have spent well over 90 seconds trying to calculate the exact value when it wasn't even being asked for.

In other cases, you may actually be able to use the options to arrive at the solution quicker than if you had tried to solve the question as you normally would. Consider the example below:

A region is defined by the two inequalities: $x - y^2 > 1 \; and \; xy > 1$. Which of the following points is in the defined region?

A. (10,3)
B. (10,2)
C. (-10,3)
D. (-10,2)
E. (-10,-3)

Whilst it's possible to solve this question both algebraically or graphically by manipulating the identities, by far **the quickest way is to actually use the options**. Note that options C, D and E violate the second inequality, narrowing down to answer to either A or B. For A: $10 - 3^2 = 1$ and thus this point is on the boundary of the defined region and not actually in the region. Thus the answer is B (as $10-4 = 6 > 1$.)

In general, it pays dividends to look at the options briefly and see if they can be help you arrive at the question more quickly. Get into this habit early – it may feel unnatural at first but it's guaranteed to save you time in the long run.

Keywords

If you're stuck on a question; pay particular attention to the options that contain key modifiers like "**always**", "**only**", "**all**" as examiners like using them to test if there are any gaps in your knowledge. E.g. the statement "arteries carry oxygenated blood" would normally be true; "All arteries carry oxygenated blood" would be false because the pulmonary artery carries deoxygenated blood.

SECTION 1

Section 1 tests Maths & Physics aptitude. The questions are split approximately evenly between GCSE level and A level. You have to answer 54 questions 80 minutes making this is a very time pressured section.

The questions can be quite difficult and it's easy to get bogged down. The intense time pressure of having to do one question every 90 seconds makes this a difficult section.

Gaps in Knowledge

In addition to GCSE level physics and maths, you are also expected to have a firm command of A-level topics. This can be a problem if you haven't studied these topics at school yet. A summary of the specification is provided later in the book but you are highly advised to go through the official ENGAA Specification and ensure that you have covered all examinable topics. An electronic copy of this can be obtained from **www.uniadmissions.co.uk/ENGAA**.

The questions in this book will help highlight any particular areas of weakness or gaps in your knowledge that you may have. Upon discovering these, make sure you take some time to revise these topics before carrying on – there is little to be gained by attempting questions with huge gaps in your knowledge.

Maths

Being confident with maths is extremely important for the ENGAA. Many students find that improving their numerical and algebraic skills usually results in big improvements in their section 1 and 2 scores. Maths pervades the ENGAA so if you find yourself consistently running out of time in practice papers, spending a few hours on brushing up your basic maths skills may do wonders for you.

~ 15 ~

SECTION 1: Physics

Physics Syllabus

➤ Calculate, manipulate and resolve Vectors and their components & resultants

➤ Calculate the moment of a force

➤ Difference between normal and frictional components of contact forces

➤ Concept of 'Limiting Equilibrium'

➤ Understand how to use the coefficient of Friction including $F = \mu R$ and $F \leq \mu R$

➤ Use of the equations of Motion

➤ Graphical interpretations of vectors + scalars

➤ Derivation + Integration of physical values e.g. Velocity from an acceleration-time graph

➤ Principle of conservation of momentum (including coalescence)+ Linear Momenum

➤ Principle of conservation of energy and its application to kinetic/gravitational potential energy

➤ Application of Newton's laws e.g.
   ○ Linear Motion of point masses
   ○ Modelling of objects moving vertically or on a plante
   ○ Objects connected by a rod or pulleys

Top tip! Knowing SI units is extremely useful because they allow you to **'work out' equations** if you ever forget them e.g. The units for density are kg/m^3. Since Kg is the SI unit for mass, and m^3 is represented by volume –the equation for density must be = Mass/Volume.

This can also work the other way, for example we know that the unit for Pressure is Pascal (Pa). But based on the fact that Pressure = Force/Area, a Pascal must be equivalent to N/m^2.

Multi-Step Questions

Most ENGAA physics questions require two step calculations. Consider the example:

A metal ball is released from the roof a 20 metre building. Assuming air resistance equals is negligible; calculate the velocity at which the ball hits the ground. [$g = 10ms^{-2}$]

A. 5 ms^{-1} C. 15 ms^{-1} E. 25 ms^{-1}
B. 10 ms^{-1} D. 20 ms^{-1}

When the ball hits the ground, all of its gravitational potential energy has been converted to kinetic energy. Thus, $E_p = E_k$:

$$mg\Delta h = \frac{mv^2}{2}$$

Thus, $v = \sqrt{2gh} = \sqrt{2 \times 10 \times 20}$

$$= \sqrt{400} = 20ms^{-1}$$

Here, you were required to not only recall two equations but apply and rearrange them very quickly to get the answer; all in under 60 seconds. Thus, it is easy to understand why the physics questions are generally much harder than the biology and chemistry ones.

Note that if you were comfortable with basic Newtonian mechanics, you could have also solved this using a single suvat equation: $v^2 = u^2 + 2as$

$$v = \sqrt{2 \times 10 \times 20} = 20ms^{-1}$$

SI Units

Remember that in order to get the correct answer you must always work in SI units i.e. do your calculations in terms of metres (not centimetres) and kilograms (not grams), etc.

Formulas you MUST know:

Equations of Motion:

- $s = ut + 0.5at^2$
- $v = u + at$
- $a = (v-u)/t$
- $v^2 = u^2 + 2as$

Equations Relating to Force:
- Force = mass x acceleration
- Force = Momentum/Time
- Pressure = Force / Area
- Moment of a Force = Force x Distance
- Work done = Force x Displacement

Mechanics & Motion:
- Conservation of momentum $\Delta mv = 0$
- Force $F = \frac{\Delta mv}{t}$
- Angular velocity $\omega = \frac{v}{r} = 2\pi f$

Gravitational forces
- Force $F = \frac{Gm_1m_2}{r^2} = \frac{GMm}{r^2}$
- Potential $V = \frac{Gm}{r}$
- Acceleration $a = \frac{GM}{r^2} = \frac{\partial V}{\partial r}$

Simple harmonic motion & oscillations
- Displacement $x = ACos(2\pi ft)$
- Acceleration $a = -(2\pi f)^2 x = -(2\pi f)^2 ACos(2\pi ft)$
- Speed $v = \pm 2\pi f\sqrt{A^2 - x^2}$

Equations relating to Energy:
- Kinetic Energy = $0.5\ mv^2$
- Δ in Gravitational Potential Energy = $mg\Delta h$
- Energy Efficiency = (Useful energy/ Total energy) x 100%

Equations relating to Power:
- Power = Work done / time
- Power = Energy transferred / time
- Power = Force x velocity

For objects in equilibrium:
- Sum of Clockwise moments = Sum of Anti-clockwise moments
- Sum of all resultant forces = 0

Electrical Equations:
- $Q = It$
- $V = IR$
- $P = IV = I^2R = V^2/R$
- emf $\varepsilon = \frac{E}{Q} = I(R + r)$
- Resistivity $\rho = \frac{RA}{l}$
- Resistors in series $R = \sum_{i=1}^{n} R_i$
- Resistors in parallel s $R = \sum_{i=1}^{n} \frac{1}{R_i}$

Magnetic Fields:
- Magnetic flux $\emptyset = BA$
- Magnetic flux linkage $\emptyset N = BAN$
- Magnitude of induced emf $\varepsilon = N\frac{\Delta\emptyset}{\Delta t}$

For Transformers: $\frac{V_p}{V_s} = \frac{n_p}{n_s}$ where:

- V: Potential difference
- n: Number of turns
- p: Primary
- s: Secondary

Waves

➢ Speed $c = f\,\lambda$

➢ Period $T = \frac{1}{f}$

➢ Snell's law $n_1 sin\theta_1 = n_2 sin\theta_2$

Radioactivity

➢ Decay $N = N_0 e^{-\lambda t}$

➢ Half life $T_{1/2} = \frac{ln2}{\lambda}$

➢ Activity $A = \lambda N$

➢ Energy $E = mc^2$

Other:

➢ Weight = mass x g

➢ Density = Mass / Volume

➢ Momentum = Mass x Velocity

➢ $g = 9.81$ ms^{-2} (unless otherwise stated)

Factor	Text	Symbol
10^{12}	Tera	T
10^{9}	Giga	G
10^{6}	Mega	M
10^{3}	Kilo	k
10^{2}	Hecto	h
10^{-1}	Deci	d
10^{-2}	Centi	c
10^{-3}	Milli	m
10^{-6}	Micro	μ
10^{-9}	Nano	n
10^{-12}	Pico	p

Physics Questions

Question 1:
Which of the following statements are **FALSE**?

A. Electromagnetic waves cause things to heat up.
B. X-rays and gamma rays can knock electrons out of their orbits.
C. Loud sounds can make objects vibrate.
D. Wave power can be used to generate electricity.
E. Since waves carry energy away, the source of a wave loses energy.
(F) The amplitude of a wave determines its mass.

Question 2:
A spacecraft is analysing a newly discovered exoplanet. A rock of unknown mass falls on the planet from a height of 30 m. Given that g = 5.4 ms^{-2} on the planet, calculate the speed of the rock when it hits the ground and the time it took to fall.

	Speed (ms^{-1})	Time (s)
(A)	18	3.3
B	18	3.1
C	12	3.3
D	10	3.7
E	9	2.3
F	1	0.3

Question 3:

A canoe floating on the sea rises and falls 7 times in 49 seconds. The waves pass it at a speed of 5 ms^{-1}. How long are the waves?

A. 12 m   C. 25 m   E. 57 m
B. 22 m   D. 35 m   F. 75 m

Question 4:

Miss Orrell lifts her 37.5 kg bike for a distance of 1.3 m in 5 s. The acceleration of free fall is 10 ms^{-2}. What is the average power that she develops?

A. 9.8 W   C. 57.9 W   E. 97.5W
B. 12.9 W   D. 79.5 W   F. 98.0 W

Question 5:

A truck accelerates at 5.6 ms^{-2} from rest for 8 seconds. Calculate the final speed and the distance travelled in 8 seconds.

	Final Speed (ms^{-1})	Distance (m)
A	40.8	119.2
B	40.8	129.6
C	42.8	179.2
D	44.1	139.2
E	44.1	179.7
F	44.2	129.2
G	44.8	179.2
H	44.8	179.7

Question 6:
Which of the following statements is true when a sky diver jumps out of a plane?

A. The sky diver leaves the plane and will accelerate until the air resistance is greater than their weight.
B. The sky diver leaves the plane and will accelerate until the air resistance is less than their weight.
C. The sky diver leaves the plane and will accelerate until the air resistance equals their weight.
D. The sky diver leaves the plane and will accelerate until the air resistance equals their weight squared.
E. The sky diver will travel at a constant velocity after leaving the plane.

Question 7:
A 100 g apple falls on Isaac's head from a height of 20 m. Calculate the apple's momentum before the point of impact. Take $g = 10$ ms^{-2}

A. 0.1 kgms^{-1} C. 1 kgms^{-1} E. 10 kgms^{-1}
B. 0.2 kgms^{-1} D. 2 kgms^{-1} F. 20 kgms^{-1}

Question 8:
Which of the following do all electromagnetic waves all have in common?

1. They can travel through a vacuum.
2. They can be reflected.
3. They are the same length.
4. They have the same amount of energy.
5. They can be polarised.

A. 1, 2 and 3 only   D. 3 and 4 only
B. 1, 2, 3 and 4 only   E. 1, 2 and 5 only
C. 4 and 5 only   F. 1 and 5 only

Question 9:

A battery with an internal resistance of 0.8 Ω and e.m.f of 36 V is used to power a drill with resistance 1 Ω. What is the current in the circuit when the drill is connected to the power supply?

A. 5 A   C. 15 A   E. 25 A
B. 10 A   (D) 20 A   F. 30 A

Question 10:

Officer Bailey throws a 20 g dart at a speed of 100 ms^{-1}. It strikes the dartboard and is brought to rest in 10 milliseconds. Calculate the average force exerted on the dart by the dartboard.

A. 0.2 N   C. 20 N   E. 2,000 N
B. 2 N   (D) 200 N   F. 20,000 N

Question 11:

Professor Huang lifts a 50 kg bag through a distance of 0.7 m in 3 s. What average power does she develop to 3 significant figures? Take $g = 10$ms^{-2}

A. 112 W   D. 115 W
B. 113 W   E. 116 W
C. 114 W   (F) 117 W

Question 12:

An electric scooter is travelling at a speed of 30 ms^{-1} and is kept going against a 50 N frictional force by a driving force of 300 N in the direction of motion. Given that the engine runs at 200 V, calculate the current in the scooter.

A. 4.5 A   D. 4,500 A
(B) 45 A   E. 45,000 A
C. 450 A   F. More information needed.

Question 13:

Which of the following statements about the physical definition of work are correct?

1. $Work\ done = \frac{Force}{distance}$
2. The unit of work is equivalent to $Kgms^{-2}$.
3. Work is defined as a force causing displacement of the body upon which it acts.

A. Only 1	D. 1 and 2
B. Only 2	E. 2 and 3
C. Only 3	F. 1 and 3

Question 14:

Which of the following statements about kinetic energy are correct?

1. It is defined as $E_k = \frac{mv^2}{2}$
2. The unit of kinetic energy is equivalent to $Pa \times m^3$.
3. Kinetic energy is equal to the amount of energy needed to decelerate the body in question from its current speed.

A. Only 1	D. 1 and 2	G. 1, 2 and 3
B. Only 2	E. 2 and 3	
C. Only 3	F. 1 and 3	

Question 15:

In relation to radiation, which of the following statements is **FALSE**?

A. Radiation is the emission of energy in the form of waves or particles.
B. Radiation can be either ionizing or non-ionizing.
C. Gamma radiation has very high energy.
D. Alpha radiation is of higher energy than beta radiation.
E. X-rays are an example of wave radiation.

Question 16:

In relation to the physical definition of half-life, which of the following statements are correct?

1. In radioactive decay, the half-life is independent of atom type and isotope.
2. Half-life is defined as the time required for exactly half of the entities to decay.
3. Half-life applies to situations of both exponential and non-exponential decay.

A. Only 1   C. Only 3   E. 2 and 3
B. Only 2   D. 1 and 2   F. 1 and 3

Question 17:

In relation to nuclear fusion, which of the following statements is **FALSE**?

A. Nuclear fusion is initiated by the absorption of neutrons.
B. Nuclear fusion describes the fusion of hydrogen atoms to form helium atoms.
C. Nuclear fusion releases great amounts of energy.
D. Nuclear fusion requires high activation temperatures.
E. All of the statements above are false.

Question 18:

In relation to nuclear fission, which of the following statements is correct?

A. Nuclear fission is the basis of many nuclear weapons.
B. Nuclear fission is triggered by the shooting of neutrons at unstable atoms.
C. Nuclear fission can trigger chain reactions.
D. Nuclear fission commonly results in the emission of ionizing radiation.
E. All of the above.

Question 19:
Two identical resistors (R_a and R_b) are connected in a series circuit. Which of the following statements are true?

1. The current through both resistors is the same.
2. The voltage through both resistors is the same.
3. The voltage across the two resistors is given by Ohm's Law.

A. Only 1
B. Only 2
C. Only 3
D. 1 and 2
E. 2 and 3

F. 1 and 3
G. 1, 2 and 3
H. None of the statements are true.

Question 20:
The Sun is 8 light-minutes away from the Earth. Estimate the circumference of the Earth's orbit around the Sun. Assume that the Earth is in a circular orbit around the Sun. Speed of light = 3×10^8 ms^{-1}

A. 10^{24} m
B. 10^{21} m

C. 10^{18} m
D. 10^{15} m

E. 10^{12} m
F. 10^9 m

Question 21:
Which of the following statements are true?

1. Speed is the same as velocity.
2. The internationally standardised unit for speed is ms^{-2}.
3. Velocity = distance/time.

A. Only 1
B. Only 2
C. Only 3
D. 1 and 2
E. 2 and 3

F. 1 and 3
G. 1, 2 and 3
H. None of the statements are true.

Question 22:

Which of the following statements best defines Ohm's Law?

A. The current through an insulator between two points is indirectly proportional to the potential difference across the two points.
B. The current through an insulator between two points is directly proportional to the potential difference across the two points.
C. The current through a conductor between two points is inversely proportional to the potential difference across the two points.
D. The current through a conductor between two points is proportional to the square of the potential difference across the two points.
E. The current through a conductor between two points is directly proportional to the potential difference across the two points.

Question 23:

Which of the following statements regarding Newton's Second Law are correct?

1. For objects at rest, Resultant Force must be 0 Newtons
2. Force = Mass x Acceleration
3. Force = Rate of change of Momentum

A. Only 1   E. 2 and 3
B. Only 2   F. 1 and 3
C. Only 3   G. 1, 2 and 3
D. 1 and 2

Question 24:

Which of the following equations concerning electrical circuits are correct?

1. $Charge = \dfrac{Voltage \times time}{Resistance}$

2. $Charge = \dfrac{Power \times time}{Voltage}$

3. $Charge = \dfrac{Current \times time}{Resistance}$

A. Only 1
B. Only 2
C. Only 3
D. 1 and 2
E. 2 and 3

F. 1 and 3
G. 1, 2 and 3
H. None of the equations are correct.

Question 25:
An elevator has a mass of 1,600 kg and is carrying passengers that have a combined mass of 200 kg. A constant frictional force of 4,000 N retards its motion upward. What force must the motor provide for the elevator to move with an upward acceleration of 1 ms^{-2}? Assume: $g = 10$ ms^{-2}

A. 1,190 N
B. 11,900 N

C. 18,000 N
D. 22,000 N

E. 23,800 N

Question 26:
A 1,000 kg car accelerates from rest at 5 ms^{-2} for 10 s. Then, a braking force is applied to bring it to rest within 20 seconds. What distance has the car travelled?

A. 125 m
B. 250 m
C. 650 m
D. 750 m

E. 1,200 m
F. More information needed

Question 27:
An electric heater is connected to 120 V mains by a copper wire that has a resistance of 8 ohms. What is the power of the heater?

A.	90 W		E.	9,000W
B.	180 W		F.	18,000 W
C.	900 W	*No time*	G.	More information needed.
D.	1800 W			

Question 28:
In a particle accelerator electrons are accelerated through a potential difference of 40 MV and emerge with an energy of 40MeV (1 MeV = 1.60 x 10^{-13} J). Each pulse contains 5,000 electrons and constitutes a current of 250 μA. The current is zero between pulses. Assuming that the electrons have zero energy prior to being accelerated what is the power delivered by the electron beam?

No time

A.	1 kW		D.	1,000 kW
B.	10 kW		E.	10,000 kW
C.	100 kW		F.	More information needed

Question 29:
Which of the following statements is true?

A. When an object is in equilibrium with its surroundings, there is no energy transferred to or from the object and so its temperature remains constant.
B. When an object is in equilibrium with its surroundings, it radiates and absorbs energy at the same rate and so its temperature remains constant.
C. Radiation is faster than convection but slower than conduction.
D. Radiation is faster than conduction but slower than convection.
E. None of the above.

Question 30:
A 6kg block is pulled from rest along a horizontal frictionless surface by a constant horizontal force of 12 N. Calculate the speed of the block after it has moved 300 cm.

A. $2\sqrt{3}\ ms^{-1}$

B. $4\sqrt{3}\ ms^{-1}$

C. $4\sqrt{3}\ ms^{-1}$

D. $12\ ms^{-1}$

E. $\sqrt{\frac{3}{2}}\ ms^{-1}$

Question 31:
A 100 V heater heats 1.5 litres of pure water from 10°C to 50°C in 50 minutes. Given that 1 kg of pure water requires 4,000 J to raise its temperature by 1°C, calculate the resistance of the heater.

A. 12.5 ohms

B. 25 ohms

C. 125 ohms

D. 250 ohms

E. 500 ohms

F. 850 ohms

Question 32:
Which of the following statements are true?

1. Nuclear fission is the basis of nuclear energy.
2. Following fission, the resulting atoms are a different element to the original one.
3. Nuclear fission often results in the production of free neutrons and photons.

A. Only 1

B. Only 2

C. Only 3

D. 1 and 2

E. 2 and 3

F. 1 and 3

G. 1, 2 and 3

H. None of the statements are true

~ 31 ~

Question 33:

Which of the following statements are true? Assume $g = 10$ ms^{-2}.

1. Gravitational potential energy is defined as $E_p = m \times g \times \Delta h$.
2. Gravitational potential energy is a measure of the work done against gravity.
3. A reservoir situated 1 km above ground level with 10^6 litres of water has a potential energy of 1 Giga Joule.

A. Only 1	F. 1 and 3
B. Only 2	G. 1, 2 and 3
C. Only 3	H. None of the statements are true
D. 1 and 2	
E. 2 and 3	

Question 34:

Which of the following statements are correct in relation to Newton's 3rd law?

1. For every action there is an equal and opposite reaction.
2. According to Newton's 3rd law, there are no isolated forces.
3. Rockets cannot accelerate in deep space because there is nothing to generate an equal and opposite force.

A. Only 1	C. Only 3	E. 2 and 3
B. Only 2	D. 1 and 2	F. 1 and 3

Question 35:

Which of the following statements are correct?
1. Positively charged objects have gained electrons.
2. Electrical charge in a circuit over a period of time can be calculated if the voltage and resistance are known.
3. Objects can be charged by friction.

A. Only 1
B. Only 2
C. Only 3
D. 1 and 2

E. 2 and 3
F. 1 and 3
G. 1, 2 and 3

Question 36:
Which of the following statements is true?

A. The gravitational force between two objects is independent of their mass.
B. Each planet in the solar system exerts a gravitational force on the Earth.
C. For satellites in a geostationary orbit, acceleration due to gravity is equal and opposite to the lift from engines.
D. Two objects that are dropped from the Eiffel tower will always land on the ground at the same time if they have the same mass.
E. All of the above.
F. None of the above.

Question 37:
Which of the following best defines an electrical conductor?

 A. Conductors are usually made from metals and they conduct electrical charge in multiple directions.

B. Conductors are usually made from non-metals and they conduct electrical charge in multiple directions.

C. Conductors are usually made from metals and they conduct electrical charge in one fixed direction.

D. Conductors are usually made from non-metals and they conduct electrical charge in one fixed direction.

E. Conductors allow the passage of electrical charge with zero resistance because they contain freely mobile charged particles.

F. Conductors allow the passage of electrical charge with maximal resistance because they contain charged particles that are fixed and static.

Question 38:
An 800 kg compact car delivers 20% of its power output to its wheels. If the car has a mileage of 30 miles/gallon and travels at a speed of 60 miles/hour, how much power is delivered to the wheels? 1 gallon of petrol contains 9×10^8 J.

A.   10 kW
B.   20 kW
C.   40 kW

D.   50 kW
E.   100 kW

Question 39:
Which of the following statements about beta radiation are true?

1. After a beta particle is emitted, the atomic mass number is unchanged.
2. Beta radiation can penetrate paper but not aluminium foil.
3. A beta particle is emitted from the nucleus of the atom when an electron changes into a neutron.

A. 1 only   C. 1 and 3   E. 2 and 3
B. 2 only   D. 1 and 2   F. 1, 2 and 3

Question 40:

A car with a weight of 15,000 N is travelling at a speed of 15 ms^{-1} when it crashes into a wall and is brought to rest in 10 milliseconds. Calculate the average braking force exerted on the car by the wall. Take $g = 10$ ms^{-2}

A. $1.25 \times 10^4 N$ C. $1.25 \times 10^6 N$ E. $2.25 \times 10^5 N$
B. $1.25 \times 10^5 N$ D. $2.25 \times 10^4 N$ F. $2.25 \times 10^6 N$

Question 41:
Which of the following statements are correct?

1. Electrical insulators are usually metals e.g. copper.
2. The flow of charge through electrical insulators is extremely low.
3. Electrical insulators can be charged by rubbing them together.

A. Only 1   D. 1 and 2   G. 1, 2 and 3
B. Only 2   E. 2 and 3
C. Only 3   F. 1 and 3

The following information is needed for Questions 42 and 43:

The graph below represents a car's movement. At t=0 the car's displacement was 0 m.

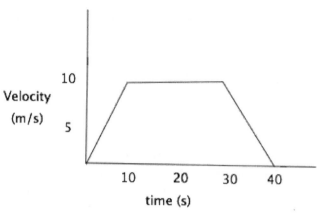

Question 42:

Which of the following statements are not true?

1. The car is reversing after t = 30.
2. The car moves with constant acceleration from t = 0 to t = 10.
3. The car moves with constant speed from t = 10 to t = 30.

A. 1 only   D. 1 and 3   G. 1, 2 and 3
B. 2 only   E. 1 and 2
C. 3 only   F. 2 and 3

Question 43:

Calculate the distance travelled by the car.

A. 200 m   D. 400 m
B. 300 m   E. 500 m
C. 350 m   F. More information needed

Question 44:

A 1,000 kg rocket is launched during a thunderstorm and reaches a constant velocity 30 seconds after launch. Suddenly, a strong gust of wind acts on it for 5 seconds with a force of 10,000 N in the direction of movement. What is the resulting change in velocity?

A. 0.5 ms^{-1}

B. 5 ms^{-1}

C. 50 ms^{-1}

D. 500 ms^{-1}

E. 5000 ms^{-1}

F. More information needed

Question 45:
A 0.5 tonne crane lifts a 0.01 tonne wardrobe by 100 cm in 5,000 milliseconds.
Calculate the average power developed by the crane. Take $g = 10 \text{ ms}^{-2}$.

A. 0.2 W

B. 2 W

C. 5 W

D. 20 W

E. 50 W

F. More information needed

Question 46:
A 20 V battery is connected to a circuit consisting of a 1 Ω and 2 Ω resistor in parallel. Calculate the overall current of the circuit.

A. 6.67 A

B. 8 A

C. 10 A

D. 12 A

E. 20 A

F. 30 A

Question 47:
Which of the following statements is correct?

A. The speed of light changes when it enters water.
B. The speed of light changes when it leaves water.
C. The direction of light changes when it enters water.
D. The direction of light changes when it leaves water.
E. All of the above.
F. None of the above.

Question 48:
In a parallel circuit, a 60 V battery is connected to two branches. Branch A contains 6 identical 5 Ω resistors and branch B contains 2 identical 10 Ω resistors. $30\,\Omega$ $20\,\Omega$

Calculate the current in branches A and B. $V = IR$ $I = \frac{V}{R}$

	I_A (A)	I_B (A)
A	0	6
B	6	0
C	2	3
D	3	2
E	3	3
F	1	5
G	5	1

Question 49:
Calculate the voltage of an electrical circuit that has a power output of 50,000,000,000 nW and a current of 0.000000004 GA.

A. 0.0125 GV
B. 0.0125 MV
C. 0.0125 kV
D. 0.0125 V

E. 0.0125 mV
F. 0.0125 μV
G. 0.0125 nV

Question 50:
Which of the following statements about radioactive decay is correct?

A. Radioactive decay is highly predictable.
B. An unstable element will continue to decay until it reaches a stable nuclear configuration.
C. All forms of radioactive decay release gamma rays.
D. All forms of radioactive decay release X-rays.
E. An atom's nuclear charge is unchanged after it undergoes alpha decay.
F. None of the above.

Question 51:
A circuit contains three identical resistors of unknown resistance connected in series with a 15 V battery. The power output of the circuit is 60 W.
Calculate the overall resistance of the circuit when two further identical resistors are added to it.

A. 0.125 Ω
B. 1.25 Ω
C. 3.75 Ω

D. 6.25 Ω
E. 18.75 Ω
F. More information needed.

Question 52:

A 5,000 kg tractor's engine uses 1 litre of fuel to move 0.1 km. 1 ml of the fuel contains 20 kJ of energy.

Calculate the engine's efficiency. Take $g = 10 \text{ ms}^{-2}$

A. 2.5 %

B. 25 %

C. 38 %

D. 50 %

E. 75 %

F. More information needed.

Question 53:

Which of the following statements are correct?

1. Electromagnetic induction occurs when a wire moves relative to a magnet.
2. Electromagnetic induction occurs when a magnetic field changes.
3. An electrical current is generated when a coil rotates in a magnetic field.

A. Only 1

B. Only 2

C. Only 3

D. 1 and 2

E. 2 and 3

F. 1 and 3

G. 1, 2 and 3

Question 54:
Which of the following statements are correct regarding parallel circuits?
1. The current flowing through a branch is dependent on the branch's resistance.
2. The total current flowing into the branches is equal to the total current flowing out of the branches.
3. An ammeter will always give the same reading regardless of its location in the circuit.

A. Only 1   E. 2 and 3
B. Only 2   F. 1 and 3
C. Only 3   G. All of the above
D. 1 and 2

Question 55:
Which of the following statements regarding series circuits are true?
1. The overall resistance of a circuit is given by the sum of all resistors in the circuit.
2. Electrical current moves from the positive terminal to the negative terminal.
3. Electrons move from the positive terminal to the negative terminal.

A. Only 1   D. 1 and 2
B. Only 2   E. 2 and 3
C. Only 3   F. 1 and 3

Question 56:

The graphs below show current vs. voltage plots for 4 different electrical components.

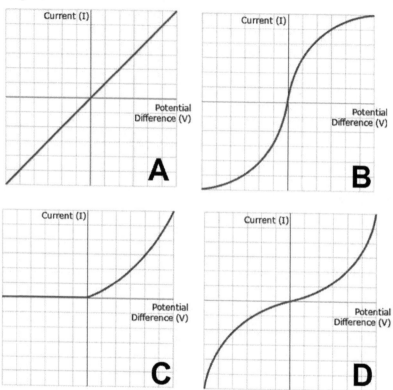

Which of the following graphs represents a resistor at constant temperature, and which a filament lamp?

	Fixed Resistor	Filament Lamp
A	A	B
B	A	C
C	A	D
D	C	A
E	C	C
F	C	D

Question 57:
Which of the following statements are true about vectors?

A. Vectors can be added or subtracted.
B. All vector quantities have a defined magnitude.
C. All vector quantities have a defined direction.
D. Displacement is an example of a vector quantity.
E. All of the above.
F. None of the above.

Question 58:
The acceleration due to gravity on the Earth is six times greater than that on the moon. Dr Tyson records the weight of a rock as 250 N on the moon.

Calculate the rock's density given that it has a volume of 250 cm³. Take $g_{Earth} = 10$ ms^{-2}

A. 0.2 kg/cm³
B. 0.5 kg/cm³
C. 0.6 kg/cm³

D. 0.7 kg/cm³
E. 0.8 kg/cm³
F. More information needed.

Question 59:

A radioactive element X_{78}^{225} undergoes alpha decay. What is the atomic mass and atomic number after 5 alpha particles have been released?

	Mass Number	Atomic Number
A	200	56
B	200	58
C	205	64
D	205	68
E	215	58
F	215	73
G	225	78
H	225	83

Question 60:

A 20 A current passes through a circuit with resistance of 10 Ω. The circuit is connected to a transformer that contains a primary coil with 5 turns and a secondary coil with 10 turns. Calculate the potential difference exiting the transformer.

A. 100 V
B. 200 V
C. 400 V
D. 500 V

E. 2,000 V
F. 4,000 V
G. 5,000 V

Question 61:

A metal sphere of unknown mass is dropped from an altitude of 1 km and reaches terminal velocity 300 m before it hits the ground. Given that resistive forces do a total of 10 kJ of work for the last 100 m before the ball hits the ground, calculate the mass of the ball. Take $g = 10\text{ms}^{-2}$.

A. 1 kg
B. 2 kg
C. 5 kg

D. 10 kg
E. 20 kg
F. More information needed.

Question 62:

Which of the following statements is true about the electromagnetic spectrum?

A. The wavelength of ultraviolet waves is shorter than that of x-rays.
B. For waves in the electromagnetic spectrum, wavelength is directly proportional to frequency.
C. Most electromagnetic waves can be stopped with a thin layer of aluminium.
D. Waves in the electromagnetic spectrum travel at the speed of sound.
E. Humans are able to visualise the majority of the electromagnetic spectrum.
F. None of the above.

Question 63:

In relation to the Doppler Effect, which of the following statements are true?

1. If an object emitting a wave moves towards the sensor, the wavelength increases and frequency decreases. ✗
2. An object that originally emitted a wave of a wavelength of 20 mm followed by a second reading delivering a wavelength of 15 mm is moving towards the sensor.
3. The faster the object is moving away from the sensor, the greater the increase in frequency. ✗

A. Only 1	F. 2 and 3
B. Only 2	G. 1, 2 and 3
C. Only 3	H. None of the above statements
D. 1 and 2	are true.
E. 1 and 3	

Question 64:

A 5 g bullet is travels at 1 km/s and hits a brick wall. It penetrates 50 cm before being brought to rest 100 ms after impact. Calculate the average braking force exerted by the wall on the bullet.

A. 50 N	D. 50,000 N
B. 500 N	E. 500,000 N
C. 5,000 N	F. More information needed.

~ 46 ~

Question 65:
Polonium (Po) is a highly radioactive element that has no known stable isotope. Po^{210} undergoes radioactive decay to Pb^{206} and Y. Calculate the number of protons in 10 moles of Y. [Avogadro's Constant = 6×10^{23}]

A. 0

B. 1.2×10^{24}

C. 1.2×10^{25}

D. 2.4×10^{24}

E. 2.4×10^{25}

F. More information needed

Question 66:
Dr Sale measures the background radiation in a nuclear wasteland to be 1,000 Bq. He then detects a spike of 16,000 Bq from a nuclear rod made up of an unknown material. 300 days later, he visits and can no longer detect a reading higher than 1,000 Bq from the rod, even though it hasn't been disturbed.
What is the longest possible half-life of the nuclear rod?

A. 25 days

B. 50 days

C. 75 days

D. 100 days

E. 150 days

F. More information needed

Question 67:

A radioactive element Y_{89}^{200} undergoes a series of beta (β^-) and gamma decays. What are the number of protons and neutrons in the element after the emission of 5 beta particles and 2 gamma waves?

	Protons	Neutrons
A	79	101
B	84	111
C	84	116
D	89	111
E	89	106
F	94	111
G	94	106
H	109	111

Question 68:
Most symphony orchestras tune to 'standard pitch' (frequency = 440 Hz). When they are tuning, sound directly from the orchestra reaches audience members that are 500 m away in 1.5 seconds.
Estimate the wavelength of 'standard pitch'.

A. 0.05 m

B. 0.5 m

C. 0.75 m

D. 1.5 m

E. 15 m

F. More information needed

Question 69:

A 1 kg cylindrical artillery shell with a radius of 50 mm is fired at a speed of 200 ms^{-1}. It strikes an armour plated wall and is brought to rest in 500 µs.

Calculate the average pressure exerted on the entire shell by the wall at the time of impact.

A. 5×10^6 Pa   D. 5×10^9 Pa
B. 5×10^7 Pa   E. 5×10^{10} Pa
C. 5×10^8 Pa   F. More information needed

Question 70:

A 1,000 W display fountain launches 120 litres of water straight up every minute. Given that the fountain is 10% efficient, calculate the maximum possible height that the stream of water could reach.
Assume that there is negligible air resistance and $g = 10$ ms^{-2}.

A. 1 m   D. 20 m
B. 5 m   E. 50m
C. 10 m   F. More information needed

Question 71

In relation to transformers, which of the following is true?
1. Step up transformers increase the voltage leaving the transformer.
2. In step down transformers, the number of turns in the primary coil is smaller than in the secondary coil.
3. For transformers that are 100% efficient: $I_p V_p = I_s V_s$

A. Only 1   E. 1 and 3
B. Only 2   F. 2 and 3
C. Only 3   G. 1, 2 and 3
D. 1 and 2   H. None of the above.

Question 72:
The half-life of Carbon-14 is 5,730 years. A bone is found that contains 6.25% of the amount of C^{14} that would be found in a modern one. How old is the bone?

A. 11,460 years
B. 17,190 years
C. 22,920 years

D. 28,650 years
E. 34,380 years
F. 40,110 years

Question 73:
A wave has a velocity of 2,000 mm/s and a wavelength of 250 cm. What is its frequency in MHz?

A. 8×10^{-3} MHz
B. 8×10^{-4} MHz
C. 8×10^{-5} MHz

D. 8×10^{-6} MHz
E. 8×10^{-7} MHz
F. 8×10^{-8} MHz

Question 74:
A radioactive element has a half-life of 25 days. After 350 days it has a count rate of 50. What was its original count rate?

A. 102,400
B. 162,240
C. 204,800
D. 409,600

E. 819,200
F. 1,638,400
G. 3,276,800

Question 75:
Which of the following units is **NOT** equivalent to a Volt (V)?

A. $A\Omega$
B. WA^{-1}
C. $Nms^{-1}A^{-1}$

D. NmC
E. JC^{-1}
F. $JA^{-1}s^{-1}$

Advanced Physics Questions

Question 76:

A ball is swung in a vertical circle from a string (of negligible mass). What is the minimum speed at the top of the arc for it to continue in a circular path?

A. 0

B. mgr

C. $2r^2$

D. mg

E. $\sqrt{gr}$

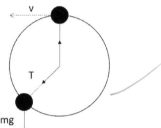

Question 77:

A person pulls on a rope at 60° to the horizontal to exert a force on a mass m as shown. What is the power needed to move the mass up the 30° incline at a constant velocity, v, given a friction force F?

A. $\left(mg + \frac{F}{2}\right)v$

B. $\frac{mg}{\sqrt{2}} - F$

C. $\left(\frac{mg}{2}\right)v$

D. $\sqrt{2}Fv$

E. $\left(\frac{mg}{2} + F\right)v$

Question 78:
What is the maximum speed of a point mass, m, suspended from a string of length l, (a pendulum) if it is released from an angle θ where the string is taught?

A. $2gl(1 - \cos(\theta))$

B. $2gl(1 - \sin(\theta))$

C. $\sqrt{2gl(1 - \cos(\theta))}$

D. $\sqrt{2gl(1 - \sin(\theta))}$

E. $\sqrt{2gl(1 - \cos^2(\theta))}$

Question 79:
Two spheres of equal mass, m, one at rest and one moving at velocity u1 towards the other as shown. After the collision, they move at angles φ and θ from the initial velocity u1 at respective velocities v_1 and v_2 where $v_2 = 2v_1$. What is the angle θ?

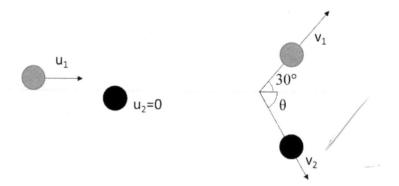

A. 0°

B. sin(50)

C. 30°

D. 45°

E. 90°

Question 80:

The first ball is three times the mass of the others. If this is an elastic collision, how many of the other ball move and at what velocity after the collision?

	Number of balls	Velocity
A	1	3v
B	1	v/3
C	3	v/3
D	3	v
E	3	$\sqrt{v}$

E lostic = Ke conserved

Question 81:

A ball is kicked over a 3 m fence from 6 m away with an initial height of zero. Assuming no air resistance what is the minimum angle the ball must leave the ground at the make it over the fence?

A. $\arctan(2)$

B. $\arctan\left(\frac{1}{2}\right)$

C. $\arcsin\left(\frac{1}{2}\right)$

D. $45°$

E. $\arccos\left(\frac{-1}{2}\right)$

Question 82:

A mass on a spring of spring constant k is in simple harmonic motion at frequency f. If the mass is halved and the spring constant is double, by what factor will the frequency of oscillation change?

A. Stay the same

B. 2

C. 4

D. $\frac{1}{2}$

E. $\sqrt{2}$

~ 53 ~

Question 83:

A ball is dropped from 3 m above the ground and rebounds to a maximum height of 1 m. How much kinetic energy does it have just before hitting the ground and at the top of its bounce, and what is the maximum speed the ball reaches in any direction?

	E_k at Bottom	E_k at Top	Max Speed
A	0	30m	$2\sqrt{15}$
B	0	30m	30
C	30m	0	$2\sqrt{15}$
D	30m	0	60
E	60m	0	60

Question 84:

An object approaches a stationary observer at a 10% of the speed of light, c. If the observer is 2 m tall, how tall will it look to the object?

A. $0.9l$

B. $1.1l$

C. l

D. $l\sqrt{0.99}$

E. $l\sqrt{1.01}$

Question 85:

What is the stopping distance of a car moving at v m/s if its breaking force is half its weight?

A. v^2

B. $\dfrac{v^2}{g}$

C. $2mv$

D. $\dfrac{v^2}{2}$

E. $\sqrt{mg}$

Question 86:
The amplitude of a wave is damped from an initial amplitude of 200 to 25 over 12 seconds. How many seconds did it take to reach half its original amplitude?

A. 1
B. 2
C. 3

D. 4
E. 6

Question 87:
Two frequencies, f and $\frac{7}{8}f$, interfere to produce beats of 10 Hz. What is the original frequency f?

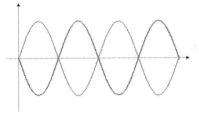

A. 11 Hz
B. 60 Hz
C. 80 Hz
D. 160 Hz
E. 200 Hz

Question 88:
The two waves represent:

A. A standing wave with both ends fixed
B. The 4th harmonic
C. Destructive interference
D. A reflection from a plane surface
E. All of the above

Question 89:

Radioactive element ^a_bX undergoes beta decay, and the product of this decay emits an alpha particle to become ^c_dY. What are the atomic number and atomic mass?

	c	d
A	a-4	b+1
B	a-3	b-2
C	a-4	b-1
D	a-5	b
E	a-1	b-4

Question 90:

A gas is heated to twice its temperature (in Kelvin) and allowed to increase in volume by 10%. What is the change in pressure?

A. 82% increase
B. 90% increase
C. 110% increase
D. 18% decrease
E. 40% decrease
F. 82% decrease

Question 91:

A beam of alpha particles enters perpendicular to the magnetic field, B, shown below coming out of the page and is deflected to follow path T. What path would a beam of electrons follow?

A. P
B. Q
C. R
D. S

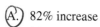

Question 92:

If all light bulbs and power supplies are identical and the joining wires have negligible resistance, which of the following light bulbs will shine brightest?

A. 1,2,3
B. 6
C. 7,8,9
D. 1,2,3,6
E. 4,5

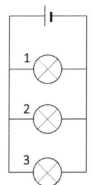
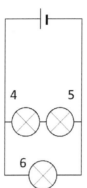
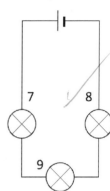

Question 93:

A convex lens with focal length f is used to create an image of object O. Where is the image formed?

A. V
B. W
C. X
D. Y
E. Z

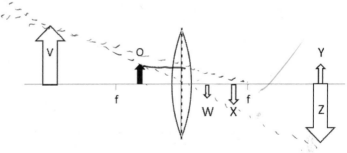

Question 94:

A flower pot hangs on the end of a rod protruding at right angles from a wall, held up by string attached two thirds of the way along. What must the tension in the string be if the rod is weightless and the system is at equilibrium?

A. $mg \sin \theta$

B. $\dfrac{3mg}{2\sin \theta}$

C. $\dfrac{3mg}{2\cos \theta}$

D. $\dfrac{2mg}{3\sin \theta}$

E. $\dfrac{2mg}{3\cos \theta}$

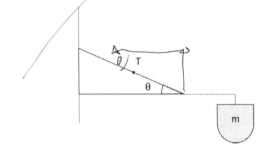

Question 95:

When a clean, negatively charged metal surface is irradiated with electromagnetic radiation of sufficient frequency, electrons are emitted. This observation describes what phenomenon and what property does the intercept on the experimental plot below represent?

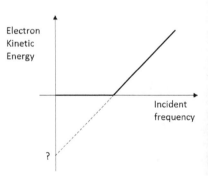

A	Photoelectric effect	Stopping potential
B	Evaporation	Stopping potential
C	Wave particle duality	Work function
D	Thermionic emission	Work function
E	Photoabsorbtion	Stopping potential

Question 96:
Which of these wave phenomena can be explained by Huygen's principle of wave propagation?

1. Diffraction
2. Refraction
3. Reflection
4. Interference
5. Damping

A. None
B. 1,2,3
C. 1,4
D. 1,2,3,4
E. All

Question 97:
What is the maximum efficiency of an engine where the isothermal expansion of a gas takes place at $T_1 = 420$ K and the reversible isothermal compression of the gas occurs at temperature $T_2 = 280$ K?

A. 43%   D. 92%
B. 57%   E. 100%
C. 75%

Question 98:
Which of the following statements is true?

A. A capacitor works based on the principle of electromagnetic induction.
B. A motor requires a AC input
C. Transformers produce DC current
D. The magnetic field produced by a current carrying wire is parallel to the direction of flow of charge.
E. A generator must have a moving wire.

Question 99:

For the logic gate below, if inputs are all set to 1, what would the value of X, Y and Z be?

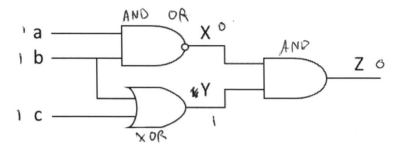

	X	**Y**	**Z**
A	0	0	0
B	0	0	1
C	0	1	0
D	1	0	0
E	1	1	1

Question 100:

What material property is given by each point P, Q and R on a stress-strain curve?

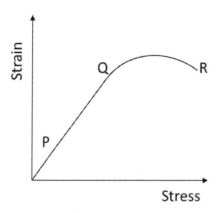

	P	Q	R
A	Elastic Modulus	Yield stress	Fracture toughness
B	Tensile Modulus	Plastic onset	Yield stress
C	Hardness	Stiffness	Ductile failure
D	Ductility	Elastic limit	Brittle fracture
E	Young's Modulus	Yield stress	Fracture stress

SECTION 1: Maths

Advanced Maths Syllabus

Algebra:
➢ Laws of Indices
➢ Manipulation of Surds
➢ Quadratic Functions: Graphs, use of discrimiant, completing the square
➢ Solving Simulatenous Equations via Substitution
➢ Solving Linear and Quadratic Inequalities
➢ Manipulation of polynomials e.g. expanding brackets, factorising
➢ Use of Factor Theorem + Remainder Theorem

Graphing Functions:
➢ Sketching of common functions including lines, quadratics, cubics, trigonometric functions, logarithmic functions and exponential functions
➢ Manipulation of functions using simple transformaions

Differentiation:
➢ First order and second order derivatives
➢ Familiarity with notation: $\frac{dy}{dx}, \frac{d^2y}{dx^2}, f'(x), f''(x)$
➢ Differentiation of functions like $y = x^n$

Integration:
➢ Definite and indefinite integrals for $y = x^n$
➢ Solving Differential Equations in the form: $\frac{dy}{dx} = f(x)$
➢ Understanding of the Fundamental Theorem of Calculus and its application:
  ○ $\int_a^b f(x)dx = F(b) - F(a), where\ F'(x) = f(x)$
  ○ $\frac{d}{dx}\int_a^x f(t)dt = f(x)$

Geometry:
➤ Circle Properties:
  ○ The angle subtended by an arc at the centre of a circle is double the size of the angle subtended by the arc on the circumference
  ○ The opposite angles in a cyclic quadrilateral summate to 180 degrees
  ○ The angle between the tanent and chord at the point of contact is equal to the angle in the alternate segment
  ○ The tangent at any point on a circle is perpendicular to the radius at that point
  ○ Triangles formed using the full diameter are right-angled triangles
  ○ Angles in the same segment are equal
  ○ The Perpendicular from the centre to a chord bisects the chord
➤ Equations for a circle:
  ○ $(x - a)^2 + (y - b)^2 = r^2$
  ○ $x^2 + y^2 + cx + dy + e = 0$
➤ Equations for a straight line:
  ○ $y - y_1 = m(x - x_1)$
  ○ $Ax + by + c = 0$

Series:
➤ Arithmetic series and Geometric Series
➤ Summing to a finite and infinite geometric series
➤ Binomial Expansions
➤ Factorials

Trignometry:
➤ Sine and Cosine rules
➤ Solution of trigonometric identities
➤ Values of sin, cost, tan for 0, 30, 45, 60 and 90 degrees
➤ Sine, Cosine, Tangent graphs, symmetries, perioditicties

Logic Arguments:

➢ Terminology: True, flase, and, or not, necessary, sufficient, for all, for some, there exists.

➢ Arguments in the format:
  ○ If A then B
  ○ A if B
  ○ A only if B
  ○ A if and only if B

Law of Lograithms

➢ $a^b = c \leftrightarrow b = log_a c$

➢ $log_a x + log_a y = log_a(xy)$

➢ $log_a x - log_a y = log_a\left(\frac{x}{y}\right)$

➢ $k\, log_a x = log_a(x^k)$

➢ $log_a \frac{1}{x} = -log_a x$

➢ $log_a a = 1$

Trignometry

➢ Sin Rule: $\frac{a}{SinA} = \frac{b}{Sin\,B} = \frac{c}{Sin\,C}$

➢ Cosine Rule: $c^2 = a^2 + b^2 - 2ab\,cosC$

➢ $Area\ of\ Triangle = \frac{1}{2}ab\sin C$

➢ $\sin^2\theta + \cos^2\theta = 1$

➢ $tan\theta = \frac{sin\theta}{cos\,\theta}$

Exponentials & Logs:

➢ Graph of $y = a^x$ series

➢ Law of Lograithms

Core Forumlas:

2D Shapes		3D Shapes		
	Area		Surface Area	Volume
Circle	πr^2	**Cuboid**	Σ of 6 faces	Length x width x height
Parallelogram	Base x Vertical height	**Cylinder**	$2\pi r^2 + 2\pi rl$	πr^2 x l
Trapezium	0.5 x h x (a+b)	**Cone**	$\pi r^2 + \pi rl$	πr^2 x (h/3)
Triangle	0.5 x base x height	**Sphere**	$4\pi r^2$	$(4/3)\pi r^3$

Even good students who are studying maths at A2 can struggle with certain ENGAA maths topics because they're usually glossed over at school. These include:

Quadratic Formula

The solutions for a quadratic equation in the form $ax^2 + bx + c = 0$ are given by: $x = \frac{-b \pm \sqrt{b^2 - 4ac}}{2a}$

Remember that you can also use the discriminant to quickly see if a quadratic equation has any solutions:

$$b^2 - 4ac < 0 \Rightarrow No\ solutions$$
$$b^2 - 4ac = 0 \Rightarrow 1\ solution$$
$$b^2 - 4ac > 2 \Rightarrow 2\ solutions$$

Completing the Square

If a quadratic equation cannot be factorised easily and is in the format $ax^2 + bx + c = 0$ then you can rearrange it into the form $a\left(x + \frac{b}{2a}\right)^2 + [c - \frac{b^2}{4a}] = 0$

This looks more complicated than it is – remember that in the ENGAA, you're extremely unlikely to get quadratic equations where $a > 1$ and the equation doesn't have any easy factors. This gives you an easier equation:

$\left(x + \frac{b}{2}\right)^2 + \left[c - \frac{b^2}{4}\right] = 0$ and is best understood with an example.

Consider: $x^2 + 6x + 10 = 0$

This equation cannot be factorised easily but note that: $x^2 + 6x - 10 = x+32-19=0$

Therefore, $x = -3 \pm \sqrt{19}$. Completing the square is an important skill – make sure you're comfortable with it.

Difference between 2 Squares

If you are asked to simplify expressions and find that there are no common factors but it involves square numbers – you might be able to factorise by using the 'difference between two squares'.

For example, $x^2 - 25$ can also be expressed as $(x + 5)(x - 5)$.

Maths Questions

Question 101:

Robert has a box of building blocks. The box contains 8 yellow blocks and 12 red blocks. He picks three blocks from the box and stacks them up high. Calculate the probability that he stacks two red building blocks and one yellow building block, in **any** order.

A. $\frac{8}{20}$ C. $\frac{11}{18}$ E. $\frac{12}{20}$

B. $\frac{44}{95}$ D. $\frac{8}{19}$ F. $\frac{35}{60}$

Question 102:

Solve $\frac{3x+5}{5} + \frac{2x-2}{3} = 18$

A. 12.11   C. 13.95   E. 19

B. 13.49   D. 14.2   F. 265

Question 103:

Solve $3x^2 + 11x - 20 = 0$

A. 0.75 and $-\frac{4}{3}$ D. 5 and $\frac{4}{3}$

B. -0.75 and $\frac{4}{3}$ E. 12 only

C. -5 and $\frac{4}{3}$ F. -12 only

Question 104:

Express $\frac{5}{x+2} + \frac{3}{x-4}$ as a single fraction.

A. $\frac{15x-120}{(x+2)(x-4)}$

D. $\frac{15}{8x}$

B. $\frac{8x-26}{(x+2)(x-4)}$

E. 24

C. $\frac{8x-14}{(x+2)(x-4)}$

F. $\frac{8x-14}{x^2-8}$

Question 105:

The value of p is directly proportional to the cube root of q. When p = 12, q = 27. Find the value of q when p = 24.

A. 32

C. 124

B. 216

B. 64

D. 128

F. 1728

Question 106:

Write 72^2 as a product of its prime factors.

A. $2^6 \times 3^4$

C. $2^4 \times 3^4$

E. $2^6 \times 3$

B. $2^6 \times 3^5$

D. 2×3^3

F. $2^3 \times 3^2$

Question 107:

Calculate: $\frac{2.302 \times 10^5 + 2.302 \times 10^2}{1.151 \times 10^{10}}$

A. 0.0000202

C. 0.00002002

E. 0.000002002

B. 0.00020002

D. 0.00000002

F. 0.000002002

Question 108:

Given that $y^2 + \mathbf{a}y + \mathbf{b} = (y + 2)^2 - 5$, find the values of **a** and **b**.

	a	b
A	-1	4
B	1	9
C	-1	-9
D	-9	1
E	4	-1
F	4	1

(handwritten: $-2^2 + 6 = -5$ $b = -1$)

Question 109:

Express $\frac{4}{5} + \frac{m-2n}{m+4n}$ as a single fraction in its simplest form:

A. $\frac{6m+6n}{5(m+4n)}$

B. $\frac{9m+26n}{5(m+4n)}$

C. $\frac{20m+6n}{5(m+4n)}$

D. $\frac{3m+9n}{5(m+4n)}$

E. $\frac{3(3m+2n)}{5(m+4n)}$

F. $\frac{6m+6n}{3(m+4n)}$

Question 110:

A is inversely proportional to the square root of B. When A = 4, B = 25.

Calculate the value of A when B = 16.

A. 0.8

B. 4

C. 5

D. 6

E. 10

F. 20

Question 111:

S, T, U and V are points on the circumference of a circle, and O is the centre of the circle.

Given that angle SVU = 89°, calculate the size of the smaller angle SOU.

A. 89°

B. 91°

C. 102°

D. 178°

E. 182°

F. 212°

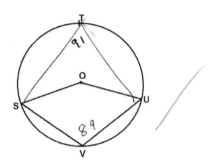

Question 112:

Open cylinder A has a surface area of 8π cm^2 and a volume of 2π cm^3. Open cylinder B is an enlargement of A and has a surface area of 32π cm^2. Calculate the volume of cylinder B.

A. 2π cm^3

B. 8π cm^3

C. 10π cm^3

D. 14π cm^3

E. 16π cm^3

F. 32π cm^3

Question 113:

Express $\dfrac{8}{x(3-x)} - \dfrac{6}{x}$ in its simplest form.

A. $\dfrac{3x-10}{x(3-x)}$

B. $\dfrac{3x+10}{x(3-x)}$

C. $\dfrac{6x-10}{x(3-2x)}$

D. $\dfrac{6x-10}{x(3+2x)}$

E. $\dfrac{6x-10}{x(3-x)}$

F. $\dfrac{6x+10}{x(3-x)}$

Question 114:

A bag contains 10 balls. 9 of those are white and 1 is black. What is the probability that the black ball is drawn in the tenth and final draw if the drawn balls are not replaced?

A. 0

B. $\frac{1}{10}$

C. $\frac{1}{100}$

D. $\frac{1}{10^{10}}$

E. $\frac{1}{362,880}$

Question 115:

Gambit has an ordinary deck of 52 cards. What is the probability of Gambit drawing 2 Kings (without replacement)?

A. 0

B. $\frac{1}{169}$

C. $\frac{1}{221}$

D. $\frac{4}{663}$

E. None of the above

Question 116:

I have two identical unfair dice, where the probability that the dice get a 6 is twice as high as the probability of any other outcome, which are all equally likely. What is the probability that when I roll both dice the total will be 12?

A. 0

B. $\frac{4}{49}$

C. $\frac{1}{9}$

D. $\frac{2}{7}$

E. None of the above

Question 117:

A roulette wheel consists of 36 numbered spots and 1 zero spot (i.e. 37 spots in total).

What is the probability that the ball will stop in a spot either divisible by 3 or 2?

A.   0

 $\frac{25}{37}$

 $\frac{25}{37}$

D. $\frac{18}{37}$

E. $\frac{24}{37}$

Question 118:

I have a fair coin that I flip 4 times. What is the probability I get 2 heads and 2 tails?

A. $\frac{1}{16}$

B. $\frac{3}{16}$

C. $\frac{3}{8}$

D. $\frac{9}{16}$

E. None of the above

Question 119:

Shivun rolls two fair dice. What is the probability that he gets a total of 5, 6 or 7?

A. $\frac{9}{36}$

B. $\frac{7}{12}$

C. $\frac{1}{6}$

D. $\frac{5}{12}$

E. None of the above

Question 120:

Dr Savary has a bag that contains x red balls, y blue balls and z green balls (and no others). He pulls out a ball, replaces it, and then pulls out another. What is the probability that he picks one red ball and one green ball?

A. $\frac{2(x+y)}{x+y+z}$

B. $\frac{xz}{(x+y+z)^2}$

C. $\frac{2xz}{(x+y+z)^2}$

D. $\frac{(x+z)}{(x+y+z)^2}$

E. $\frac{4xz}{(x+y+z)^4}$

F. More information necessary

Question 121:

Mr Kilbane has a bag that contains x red balls, y blue balls and z green balls (and no others). He pulls out a ball, does **NOT** replace it, and then pulls out another. What is the probability that he picks one red ball and one blue ball?

A. $\frac{2xy}{(x+y+z)^2}$

B. $\frac{2xy}{(x+y+z)(x+y+z-1)}$

C. $\frac{2xy}{(x+y+z)^2}$

D. $\frac{xy}{(x+y+z)(x+y+z-1)}$

E. $\frac{4xy}{(x+y+z-1)^2}$

F. More information needed

~ 73 ~

Question 122:

There are two tennis players. The first player wins the point with probability p, and the second player wins the point with probability 1-p. The rules of tennis say that the first player to score four points wins the game, unless the score is 4-3. At this point the first player to get two points ahead wins.

What is the probability that the first player wins in exactly 5 rounds?

A. $4p^4(1-p)$

B. $p^4(1-p)$

C. $4p(1-p)$

D. $4p(1-p)^4$

E. $4p^5(1-p)$

F. More information needed.

Question 123:

Solve the equation $\frac{4x+7}{2} + 9x + 10 = 7$

A. $\frac{22}{13}$

B. $-\frac{22}{13}$

C. $\frac{10}{13}$

D. $-\frac{10}{13}$

E. $\frac{13}{22}$

F. $-\frac{13}{22}$

Question 124:

The volume of a sphere is $V = \frac{4}{3}\pi r^3$, and the surface area of a sphere is $S = 4\pi r^2$. Express S in terms of V

A. $S = (4\pi)^{2/3}(3V)^{2/3}$

B. $S = (8\pi)^{1/3}(3V)^{2/3}$

C. $S = (4\pi)^{1/3}(9V)^{2/3}$

D. $S = (4\pi)^{1/3}(3V)^{2/3}$

E. $S = (16\pi)^{1/3}(9V)^{2/3}$

Question 125:

Express the volume of a cube, V, in terms of its surface area, S.

A. $V = (S/6)^{3/2}$

B. $V = S^{3/2}$

C. $V = (6/S)^{3/2}$

D. $V = (S/6)^{1/2}$

E. $V = (S/36)^{1/2}$

F. $V = (S/36)^{3/2}$

Question 126:

Solve the equations $4x + 3y = 7$ and $2x + 8y = 12$

 A. $(x, y) = \left(\frac{17}{13}, \frac{10}{13}\right)$

B. $(x, y) = \left(\frac{10}{13}, \frac{17}{13}\right)$

C. $(x, y) = (1, 2)$

D. $(x, y) = (2, 1)$

E. $(x, y) = (6, 3)$

F. $(x, y) = (3, 6)$

G. No solutions possible.

Question 127:

Rearrange $\frac{(7x+10)}{(9x+5)} = 3y^2 + 2$, to make x the subject.

 A. $\dfrac{15\,y^2}{7 - 9(3y^2+2)}$

B. $\dfrac{15\,y^2}{7 + 9(3y^2+2)}$

C. $-\dfrac{15\,y^2}{7 - 9(3y^2+2)}$

D. $-\dfrac{15\,y^2}{7 + 9(3y^2+2)}$

E. $-\dfrac{5\,y^2}{7 + 9(3y^2+2)}$

F. $\dfrac{5\,y^2}{7 + 9(3y^2+2)}$

Question 128:

Simplify $3x\left(\dfrac{3x^7}{x^{\frac{1}{3}}}\right)^3$

A. $9x^{20}$

C. $87x^{20}$

E. $27x^{21}$

B. $27x^{20}$

D. $9x^{21}$

F. $81x^{21}$

Question 129:

Simplify $2x[(2x)^7]^{\frac{1}{14}}$

A. $2x\sqrt{2\,x^4}$

C. $2\sqrt{2\,x^4}$

E. $8x^3$

B. $2x\sqrt{2x^3}$

D. $2\sqrt{2x^3}$

F. $8x$

Question 130:

What is the circumference of a circle with an area of 10π?

A. $2\pi\sqrt{10}$

D. 20π

B. $\pi\sqrt{10}$

E. $\sqrt{10}$

C. 10π

F. More information needed.

Question 131:

If $a.b = (ab) + (a+b)$, then calculate the value of $(3.4).5$

A. 19

D. 119

B. 54

E. 132

C. 100

Question 132:

If $a.b = \frac{a^b}{a}$, calculate$(2.3).2$

A. $\frac{16}{3}$

B. 1

C. 2

D. 4

E. 8

Question 133:

Solve $x^2 + 3x - 5 = 0$

A. $x = -\frac{3}{2} \pm \frac{\sqrt{11}}{2}$

B. $x = \frac{3}{2} \pm \frac{\sqrt{11}}{2}$

C. $x = -\frac{3}{2} \pm \frac{\sqrt{11}}{4}$

D. $x = \frac{3}{2} \pm \frac{\sqrt{11}}{4}$

E. $x = \frac{3}{2} \pm \frac{\sqrt{29}}{2}$

F. $x = -\frac{3}{2} \pm \frac{\sqrt{29}}{2}$

Question 134:

How many times do the curves $y = x^3$ and $y = x^2 + 4x + 14$ intersect?

A. 0

B. 1

C. 2

D. 3

E. 4

Question 135:

Which of the following graphs **do not** intersect?

1. $y = x$
2. $y = x^2$
3. $y = 1-x^2$
4. $y = 2$

A. 1 and 2

B. 2 and 3

C. 3 and 4

D. 1 and 3

E. 1 and 4

F. 2 and 4

Question 136:

Calculate the product of 897,653 and 0.009764.

A. 87646.8

B. 8764.68

C. 876.468

D. 87.6468

E. 8.76468

F. 0.876468

Question 137:

Solve for x: $\frac{7x+3}{10} + \frac{3x+1}{7} = 14$

A. $\frac{929}{51}$

B. $\frac{949}{47}$

C. $\frac{949}{79}$

D. $\frac{980}{79}$

Question 138:

What is the area of an equilateral triangle with side length x.

A. $\frac{x^2\sqrt{3}}{4}$

B. $\frac{x\sqrt{3}}{4}$

C. $\frac{x^2}{2}$

D. $\frac{x}{2}$

E. x^2

F. x

Question 139:

Simplify $3 - \frac{7x(25x^2 - 1)}{49x^2(5x+1)}$

A. $3 - \frac{5x-1}{7x}$

B. $3 - \frac{5x+1}{7x}$

C. $3 + \frac{5x-1}{7x}$

D. $3 + \frac{5x+1}{7x}$

E. $3 - \frac{5x^2}{49}$

F. $3 + \frac{5x^2}{49}$

Question 140:

Solve the equation $x^2 - 10x - 100 = 0$

A. $-5 \pm 5\sqrt{5}$

B. $-5 \pm \sqrt{5}$

C. $5 \pm 5\sqrt{5}$

D. $5 \pm \sqrt{5}$

E. $5 \pm 5\sqrt{125}$

F. $-5 \pm \sqrt{125}$

Question 141:

Rearrange $x^2 - 4x + 7 = y^3 + 2$ to make x the subject.

A. $x = 2 \pm \sqrt{y^3 + 1}$

B. $x = 2 \pm \sqrt{y^3 - 1}$

C. $x = -2 \pm \sqrt{y^3 - 1}$

D. $x = -2 \pm \sqrt{y^3 + 1}$

E. x cannot be made the subject for this equation.

Question 142:

Rearrange $3x + 2 = \sqrt{7x^2 + 2x + y}$ to make y the subject.

A. $y = 4x^2 + 8x + 2$

B. $y = 4x^2 + 8x + 4$

C. $y = 2x^2 + 10x + 2$

D. $y = 2x^2 + 10x + 4$

E. $y = x^2 + 10x + 2$

F. $y = x^2 + 10x + 4$

Question 143:

Rearrange $y^4 - 4y^3 + 6y^2 - 4y + 2 = x^5 + 7$ to make y the subject.

A. $y = 1 + (x^5 + 7)^{1/4}$

C. $y = 1 + (x^5 + 6)^{1/4}$

B. $y = -1 + (x^5 + 7)^{1/4}$

D. $y = -1 + (x^5 + 6)^{1/4}$

Question 144:

The aspect ratio of my television screen is 4:3 and the diagonal is 50 inches. What is the area of my television screen?

A. $1,200$ inches^2

D. 100 inches^2

B. $1,000$ inches^2

E. More information needed.

C. 120 inches^2

Question 145:

Rearrange the equation $\sqrt{1 + 3x^{-2}} = y^5 + 1$ to make x the subject.

A. $x = \frac{(y^{10} + 2y^5)}{3}$

E. $x = \sqrt{\frac{y^{10} + 2y^5 + 2}{3}}$

B. $x = \frac{3}{(y^{10} + 2y^5)}$

F. $x = \sqrt{\frac{3}{y^{10} + 2y^5 + 2}}$

C. $x = \sqrt{\frac{3}{y^{10} + 2y^5}}$

D. $x = \sqrt{\frac{y^{10} + 2y^5}{3}}$

Question 146:

Solve $3x - 5y = 10 \ and \ 2x + 2y = 13$.

A. $(x,y) = (\frac{19}{16}, \frac{85}{16})$

B. $(x,y) = (\frac{85}{16}, -\frac{19}{16})$

C. $(x,y) = (\frac{85}{16}, \frac{19}{16})$

D. $(x,y) = (-\frac{85}{16}, -\frac{19}{16})$

E. No solutions possible.

Question 147:

The two inequalities $x + y \leq 3 \ and \ x^3 - y^2 < 3$ define a region on a plane. Which of the following points is inside the region?

A. $(2, 1)$

B. $(2.5, 1)$

C. $(1, 2)$

D. $(3, 5)$

E. $(1, 2.5)$

F. None of the above.

Question 148:

How many times do $y = x + 4 \ and \ y = 4x^2 + 5x + 5$ intersect?

A. 0

B. 1

C. 2

D. 3

E. 4

Question 149:

How many times do $y = x^3$ and $y = x$ intersect?

A. 0

 B. 1

C. 2

D. 3

E. 4

Question 150:

A cube has unit length sides. What is the length of a line joining a vertex to the midpoint of the opposite side?

A. $\sqrt{2}$

B. $\sqrt{\frac{3}{2}}$

C. $\sqrt{3}$

D. $\sqrt{5}$

E. $\frac{\sqrt{5}}{2}$

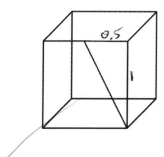

Question 151:

Solve for x, y, and z.

1. $x + y - z = -1$

2. $2x - 2y + 3z = 8$

3. $2x - y + 2z = 9$

	x	y	z
A	2	-15	-14
B	15	2	14
C	14	15	-2
D	-2	15	14
E	2	-15	14
F	No solutions possible		

Question 152:

Fully factorise: $3a^3 - 30a^2 + 75a$

A. $3a(a-3)^3$

B. $a(3a-5)^2$

C. $3a(a^2 - 10a + 25)$

D. $3a(a-5)^2$

E. $3a(a+5)^2$

Question 153:

Solve for x and y:

$4x + 3y = 48$

$3x + 2y = 34$

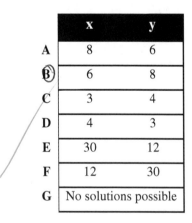

	x	y
A	8	6
B	6	8
C	3	4
D	4	3
E	30	12
F	12	30
G	No solutions possible	

Question 154:

Evaluate: $\dfrac{\cancel{-}(5^2-4\times 7)^2}{\cancel{-}6^2+2\times 7}$

A. $-\dfrac{3}{50}$

C. $-\dfrac{3}{22}$

E. $\dfrac{9}{22}$

B. $\dfrac{11}{22}$

D. $\dfrac{9}{50}$

F. 0

Question 155:

All license plates are 6 characters long. The first 3 characters consist of letters and the next 3 characters of numbers. How many unique license plates are possible?

A. 676,000

C. 67,600,000

E. 17,576,000

B. 6,760,000

D. 1,757,600

F. 175,760,000

Question 156:

How many solutions are there for: $2(2(x^2-3x)) = -9$

A. 0

D. 3

B. 1

E. Infinite solutions.

C. 2

Question 157:

Evaluate: $\left(x^{\frac{1}{2}} y^{-3}\right)^{\frac{1}{2}}$

A. $\dfrac{x^{\frac{1}{2}}}{y}$

B. $\dfrac{x}{y^{\frac{3}{2}}}$

C. $\dfrac{x^{\frac{1}{4}}}{y^{\frac{3}{2}}}$

D. $\dfrac{y^{\frac{1}{4}}}{x^{\frac{3}{2}}}$

~ 85 ~

Question 158:

Bryan earned a total of £ 1,240 last week from renting out three flats. From this, he had to pay 10% of the rent from the 1-bedroom flat for repairs, 20% of the rent from the 2-bedroom flat for repairs, and 30% from the 3-bedroom flat for repairs. The 3-bedroom flat costs twice as much as the 1-bedroom flat. Given that the total repair bill was £ 276 calculate the rent for each apartment.

	1 Bedroom	2 Bedrooms	3 Bedrooms
A	280	400	560
B	140	200	280
C	420	600	840
D	250	300	500
E	500	600	1,000

Question 159:

Evaluate: $5\,[5(6^2 - 5 \times 3) + 400^{\frac{1}{2}}]^{1/3} + 7$

A. 0

B. 25

C. 32

D. 49

E. 56

F. 200

Question 160:

What is the area of a regular hexagon with side length 1?

A. $3\sqrt{3}$

B. $\frac{3\sqrt{3}}{2}$

C. $\sqrt{3}$

D. $\frac{\sqrt{3}}{2}$

E. 6

F. More information needed

Question 161:

Dexter moves into a new rectangular room that is 19 metres longer than it is wide, and its total area is 780 square metres. What are the room's dimensions?

A. Width = 20 m; Length = -39 m ✗

B. Width = 20 m; Length = 39 m ✓

C. Width = 39 m; Length = 20 m ✗

D. Width = -39 m; Length = 20 m ✗

E. Width = -20 m; Length = 39 m ✗

Question 162:

Tom uses 34 meters of fencing to enclose his rectangular lot. He measured the diagonals to 13 metres long. What is the length and width of the lot?

A. 3 m by 4 m ✗

B. 5 m by 12 m

C. 6 m by 12 m

D. 8 m by 15 m ✓

E. 9 m by 15 m

F. 10 m by 10 m

Question 163:

Solve $\frac{3x-5}{2} + \frac{x+5}{4} = x + 1$

A. 1

B. 1.5

C. 3

D. 3.5

E. 4.5

F. None of the above

Question 164:

Calculate: $\frac{5.226 \times 10^6 + 5.226 \times 10^5}{1.742 \times 10^{10}}$

A. 0.033

B. 0.0033

C. 0.00033

D. 0.000033

E. 0.0000033

Question 165:

Calculate the area of the triangle shown to the right:

A. $3 + \sqrt{2}$

B. $\frac{2 + 2\sqrt{2}}{2}$

C. $2 + 5\sqrt{2}$

D. $3 - \sqrt{2}$

E. 3

F. 6

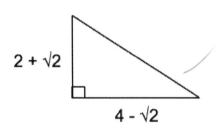

$2 + \sqrt{2}$

$4 - \sqrt{2}$

Question 166:

Rearrange $\sqrt{\dfrac{4}{x} + 9} = y - 2$ to make x the subject.

A. $x = \dfrac{11}{(y-2)^2}$

B. $x = \dfrac{9}{(y-2)^2}$

C. $x = \dfrac{4}{(y+1)(y-5)}$

D. $x = \dfrac{4}{(y-1)(y+5)}$

E. $x = \dfrac{4}{(y+1)(y+5)}$

F. $x = \dfrac{4}{(y-1)(y-5)}$

Question 167:

When 5 is subtracted from 5x the result is half the sum of 2 and 6x. What is the value of x?

A. 0

B. 1

C. 2

D. 3

E. 4

F. 6

Question 168:

Estimate $\dfrac{54.98 + 2.25^2}{\sqrt{905}}$

A. 0

B. 1

C. 2

D. 3

E. 4 ✗

F. 5

$\sqrt{4} = 2$

Question 169:

At a Pizza Parlour, you can order single, double or triple cheese in the crust. You also have the option to include ham, olives, pepperoni, bell pepper, meat balls, tomato slices, and pineapples. How many different types of pizza are available at the Pizza Parlour?

A. 10

B. 96

C. 192

D. 384

E. 768

F. None of the above

Question 170:

Solve the simultaneous equations $x^2 + y^2 = 1$ and $x + y = \sqrt{2}$, for x, y > 0

A. $(x,y) = (\frac{\sqrt{2}}{2}, \frac{\sqrt{2}}{2})$

B. $(x,y) = (\frac{1}{2}, \frac{\sqrt{3}}{2})$

C. $(x,y) = (\sqrt{2} - 1, 1)$

D. $(x,y) = (\sqrt{2}, \frac{1}{2})$

Question 171:

Which of the following statements is **FALSE**?

A. Congruent objects always have the same dimensions and shape.

B. Congruent objects can be mirror images of each other.

C. Congruent objects do not always have the same angles.

D. Congruent objects can be rotations of each other.

E. Two triangles are congruent if they have two sides and one angle of the same magnitude.

Question 172:
Solve the inequality $x^2 \geq 6 - x$

A. $x \leq -3$ and $x \leq 2$

B. $x \leq -3$ and $x \geq 2$

C. $x \geq -3$ and $x \leq 2$

D. $x \geq -3$ and $x \geq 2$

E. $x \geq 2$ only

F. $x \geq -3$ only

Question 173:
The hypotenuse of an equilateral right-angled triangle is x cm. What is the area of the triangle in terms of x?

A. $\frac{\sqrt{x}}{2}$

B. $\frac{x^2}{4}$

C. $\frac{x}{4}$

D. $\frac{3x^2}{4}$

E. $\frac{x^2}{10}$

Question 174:
Mr Heard derives a formula: $Q = \frac{(X+Y)^2 A}{3B}$. He doubles the values of X and Y, halves the value of A and triples the value of B. What happens to value of Q?

A. Decreases by $\frac{1}{3}$

B. Increases by $\frac{1}{3}$

C. Decreases by $\frac{2}{3}$

D. Increases by $\frac{2}{3}$

E. Increases by $\frac{4}{3}$

F. Decreases by $\frac{4}{3}$

Question 175:
Consider the graphs $y = x^2 - 2x + 3$, and $y = x^2 - 6x - 10$. Which of the following is true?

A. Both equations intersect the x-axis.

B. Neither equation intersects the x-axis.

C. The first equation does not intersect the x-axis; the second equation intersects the x-axis.

D. The first equation intersects the x-axis; the second equation does not intersect the x-axis.

Advanced Maths Questions

Question 176:

The vertex of an equilateral triangle is covered by a circle whose radius is half the height of the triangle. What percentage of the triangle is covered by the circle?

F.   12%
G.   16%
H.   23%
I.   33%
J.   41%
K.   50%

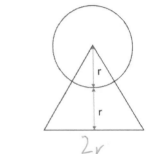

Question 177:

Three equal circles fit into a quadrilateral as shown, what is the height of the quadrilateral?

E. $2\sqrt{3}r$
G. $(2 + \sqrt{3})r$
H. $(4 - \sqrt{3})r$
I. $3r$
J. $4r$
K.   Information Needed

Question 178:
Two pyramids have equal volume and height, one with a square of side length a and one with a hexagonal base of side length b. What is the ratio of the side length of the bases?

A. $\sqrt{\dfrac{3\sqrt{3}}{2}}$

B. $\sqrt{\dfrac{2\sqrt{3}}{3}}$

C. $\sqrt{\dfrac{3}{2}}$

D. $\dfrac{2\sqrt{3}}{3}$

E. $\dfrac{3\sqrt{3}}{2}$

Question 179:
One 9 cm cube is cut into 3 cm cubes. The total surface area increases by a factor of:

A. $\dfrac{1}{3}$

B. $\sqrt{3}$

C. 3

D. 9

E. 27

Question 180:
A cone has height twice its base width (four times the circle radius). What is the cone angle (half the angle at the vertex)?

A. $30°$

B. $\sin^{-1}\left(\dfrac{r}{2}\right)$

C. $\sin^{-1}\left(\dfrac{1}{\sqrt{17}}\right)$

D. $\cos^{-1}(\sqrt{17})$

Question 181:
A hemispherical speedometer has a maximum speed of 200 mph. What is the angle travelled by the needle at a speed of 70 mph?

A. 28°   D. 88°
B. 49°   E. 92°
C. 63°

Question 182:
Two rhombuses, A and B, are similar. The area of A is 10 times that of B. What is the ratio of the smallest angles over the ratio of the shortest sides?

$$\frac{angle\ A\big/ angle\ B}{length\ A\big/ length\ B}$$

A. 0   D. $\sqrt{10}$

B. $\frac{1}{10}$ E. ∞

C. $\frac{1}{\sqrt{10}}$

Question 183:
If $f^{-1}(-x) = \ln(2x^2)$ what is $f(x)$

A. $\sqrt{\frac{e^y}{2}}$ D. $\frac{-e^y}{2}$

B. $\sqrt{\frac{e^{-y}}{2}}$ E. $\sim\sqrt{\frac{e^y}{2}}$

C. $\frac{e^y}{2}$

Question 184:
Which of the following is largest for $0 < x < 1$

A. $log_8(x)$ D. x^2

B. $log_{10}(x)$ E. $sin(x)$

C. e^x

Question 185:
x is proportional to y cubed, y is proportional to the square root of z.
$x \propto y^3, y \propto \sqrt{z}$.
If z doubles, x changes by a factor of:

A. $\sqrt{2}$ D. $\sqrt[3]{4}$

B. 2   E. 4

C. $2\sqrt{2}$

Question 186:
The area between two concentric circles (shaded) is three times that of the inner circle.

What's the size of the gap?

A. r

B. $\sqrt{2}r$

C. $\sqrt{3}r$

D. $2r$

E. $3r$

F. $4r$

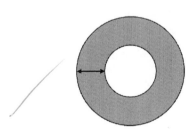

Question 187:

Solve $-x^2 \leq 3x - 4$

A. $x \geq \frac{4}{3}$

B. $1 \leq x \leq 4$

C. $x \leq 2$

D. $x \leq 1 \ or \ x \geq -4$

E. $-1 \leq x \leq \frac{3}{4}$

Question 188:

The volume of a sphere is numerically equal to its projected area. What is its radius?

A. $\frac{1}{2}$

B. $\frac{2}{3}$

C. $\frac{3}{4}$

D. $\frac{4}{3}$

E. $\frac{3}{2}$

Question 189:

What is the range where $x^2 < \frac{1}{x}$?

A. $x < 0$

B. $0 < x < 1$

C. $x > 0$

D. $x \geq 1$

E.   *None*

Question 190:

Solve $\begin{pmatrix} -1 & 2 & -1 \\ 2 & 1 & 3 \\ 2 & -1 & 4 \end{pmatrix} \begin{pmatrix} x \\ y \\ z \end{pmatrix} = \begin{pmatrix} 1 \\ 7 \\ 9 \end{pmatrix}$

A. $\begin{pmatrix} -3 \\ 0 \\ 2 \end{pmatrix}$

B. $\begin{pmatrix} 1 \\ 3 \\ 4 \end{pmatrix}$

C. $\begin{pmatrix} -2 \\ 1 \\ 3 \end{pmatrix}$

D. $\begin{pmatrix} -3 \\ 1 \\ 4 \end{pmatrix}$

E. $\begin{pmatrix} 4 \\ 2 \\ 0 \end{pmatrix}$

Question 191:

Find the value of k such that the vectors $a = -i + 6j$ and $b = 2i + kj$ are perpendicular.

A. -2

B. $-\frac{1}{3}$

C. $\frac{1}{3}$

D. 2

Question 192:

What is the perpendicular distance between point p with position vector $4i + 5j$ and the line L given by vector equation $r = -3i + j + \lambda(i + 2j)$

A. $2\sqrt{7}$

B. $5\sqrt{2}$

C. $2\sqrt{5}$

D. $7\sqrt{2}$

Question 193:

Find k such that point $\begin{pmatrix} 2 \\ k \\ -7 \end{pmatrix}$ lies within the plane $\boldsymbol{r} = \begin{pmatrix} 2 \\ 3 \\ -1 \end{pmatrix} + \lambda \begin{pmatrix} 4 \\ 1 \\ 0 \end{pmatrix} + \mu \begin{pmatrix} 2 \\ 1 \\ 3 \end{pmatrix}$

A. -2
B. -1
C. 0
D. 1
E. 2

Question 194:

What is the largest solution to $\sin(-2\theta) = 0.5$ for $\frac{\pi}{2} \le x \le 2\pi$?

A. $\frac{5\pi}{3}$ D. $\frac{7\pi}{6}$

B. $\frac{4\pi}{3}$ E. $\frac{11\pi}{6}$

C. $\frac{5\pi}{6}$

Question 195:

$\cos^4(x) - \sin^4(x) \equiv$

A. $cos(2x)$ D. $sin\ (x)cos\ (x)$
B. $2\ cos(x)$ E. $tan\ (x)$
C. $sin(2x)$

Question 196:

How many real roots does $y = 2x^5 - 3x^4 + x^3 - 4x^2 - 6x + 4$ have?

A. 1 D. 4
B. 2 E. 5
C. 3

Question 197:
What is the sum of 8 terms, $\sum_1^8 u_n$, of an arithmetic progression with $u_1 = 2$ and $d = 3$.

A. 15
B. 82
C. 100

D. 184
E. 282

Question 198:
What is the coefficient of the x^2 term in the binomial expansion of $(2 - x)5$?

A. -80
B. -48
C. 40

D. 48
E. 80

Question 199:
Given you have already thrown a 6, what is the probability of throwing three consecutive 6s using a fair die?

A. $\frac{1}{216}$
B. $\frac{1}{36}$
C. $\frac{1}{6}$

D. $\frac{1}{2}$
E. 1

Question 200:
Three people, A, B and C play darts. The probability that they hit a bullseye are respectively $\frac{1}{5}, \frac{1}{4}, \frac{1}{3}$. What is the probability that at least two shots hit the bullseye?

A. $\frac{1}{60}$ D. $\frac{1}{6}$

B. $\frac{1}{30}$ E. $\frac{3}{20}$

C. $\frac{1}{12}$

Question 201:
If probability of having blonde hair is 1 in 4, the probability of having brown eyes is 1 in 2 and the probability of having both is 1 in 8, what is the probability of having neither blonde hair nor brown eyes?

A. $\frac{1}{2}$ D. $\frac{5}{8}$

B. $\frac{3}{4}$ E. $\frac{7}{8}$

C. $\frac{3}{8}$

Question 202:
Differentiate and simplify $y = x(x + 3)^4$

A. $(x + 3)^3$
B. $(x + 3)^4$
C. $x(x + 3)^3$
D. $(x + 3)^3(5x + 3)$

Question 203:

Evaluate $\int_1^2 \frac{2}{x^2} dx$

A. -1

B. $\frac{1}{3}$

C. 1

D. $\frac{21}{4}$

E. 2

Question 204:

Express $\frac{5i}{1+2i}$ in the form $a + bi$

A. $1 + 2i$

B. $4i$

C. $1 - 2i$

D. $2 + i$

E. $5 - i$

Question 205:

Simplify $7\log_a(2) - 3\log_a(12) + 5\log_a(3)$

A. $log_{2a}(18)$

B. $log_a(18)$

C. $log_a(7)$

D. $9log_a(17)$

E. $-log_a(7)$

Question 206:

What is the equation of the asymptote of the function $y = \frac{2x^2 - x + 3}{x^2 + x - 2}$

A. $x = 0$

B. $x = 2$

C. $y = 0.5$

D. $y = 0$

E. $y = 2$

Question 207:

Find the intersection(s) of the functions $y = e^x - 3$ and $y = 1 - 3e^{-x}$

A. $0 \ and \ ln(3)$

C. $ln(4) \ and \ 1$

B. 1

D. $ln(3)$

Question 208:

Find the radius of the circle $x^2 + y^2 - 6x + 8y - 12 = 0$

A. 3

D. $\sqrt{37}$

B. $\sqrt{13}$

E. 12

C. 5

Question 209:

What value of a minimises $\int_0^a 2\sin(-x) \, dx$?

A. 0.5π

D. 3π

B. π

E. 4π

C. 2π

Question 210:

When $\dfrac{2x+3}{(x-2)(x-3)^2}$ is expressed as partial fractions, what is the numerator in the $\dfrac{A}{(x-2)}$ term:

A. -7

D. 6

B. -1

E. 7

C. 3

SECTION 2

Section 2 of the ENGAA consists of 17 MCQs normally organised into 4 groups. You are allowed access to your calculator and have 40 minutes to answer all the questions. Section 2 requires the same core knowledge as section 1.

Watch the Clock

The key to maximising your score is to have a strategy of how best to use your time. Each question is split into four parts, but not all parts are worth the same number of marks. Firstly, you should be aware of how long you should ideally be spending on each question on average. With 32 marks available this equates to around one mark per minute, but some will take longer than others. An easier goal is to think that four questions of 6-8 marks each in 40 minutes means you should spend under 10 minutes per question to (ideally) leave time for reading and checking.

Start with the 'Low Hanging Fruit'

If you see a question you know immediately how to tackle, that is where you should start. This will give you marks in the bank, leaving extra time, and will also build your confidence like a warm up lap before tackling the more challenging or unfamiliar questions. As the grouped questions follow on from each other that might mean answering the beginning of all four questions, or one question entirely, whichever you are most comfortable with. However, be warned that the more you jump around between different types of question, the more likely you are to make mistakes or waste time reacquainting yourself with the problem at hand. Once you've gone through the paper once and answered the 'obvious' questions, you can then reassess how long you have left and how many questions remain to decide how long to give each question before moving on.

Use the Question Structure

Since each question is split into four parts, its best to look ahead to the later parts of a question if you find yourself stuck on the earlier ones. These can sometimes help clarify what is expected of you at an earlier stage if you are unsure, will rely on information you have previously calculated and therefore give you a hint as to how to tackle an earlier part of the problem, remind you of a relevant formula or simply provide a clearer direction. Equally, there may be unrelated or extension questions that do not require the answers to previous sections and by not reading on you have missed out on those marks.

Proceed by Elimination

The biggest difference between the ENGAA and most other exams is that it is multiple choice. You can use this to your advantage to save time as a quick glance at the possible answers will give you more direction and understanding of what is expected of you and where to aim for. However, do not spend a long time reading all of the potential answers as this will distract you from actually solving the problem. Once you have progressed a certain way through a question, if it is obvious that you can eliminate options leaving only one possibility, there is no need to continue – you can answer the question so move on. You are not penalised for incorrect answers so there is no reason to leave the exam with any blanks. If you have run out of time, or a question is taking much longer than it should, make an educated guess and move on.

Practice

The best way to prepare is to practice not only long answer questions of this level, but also different multiple choice papers to familiarise yourself with how to eliminate options and get to the answer as fast as possible. As the exam is relatively new, there are not many past papers to use, however there are several exam boards as well as competitions like the Canadian Maths Competition that are multiple choice, which you can use for practice.

Thrive on Adversity

The ENGAA is specifically designed to be challenging and to take you out of your comfort zone. This is done in order to separate different tiers of students depending on their academic ability. The reason for this type of exam is that Cambridge attracts excellent students that will almost invariable score well in exams. If, for this reason, during your preparation, you come across questions that you find very difficult, use this as motivation to try and further your knowledge beyond the simple school syllabus. This is where the option for specialisation ties in.

Practice Calculus

Section 2 does allow you to use calculators. For this reason, practicing calculus might seem unnecessary. But it will give you a big advantage to be confident with it as you will be significantly more efficient and faster. As the math part is core knowledge for all section 2 questions, you can be certain that to some degree or other you will be required to apply your calculus.

Think in Applied Formulas

Trying to answer section 2 physics questions without first learning all the core formulas is like trying to run before you can walk – ensure you're completely confident with all the core formulas before starting the practice questions.

Variety

Physics is a very varied subject, and the questions you may be asked in an exam will reflect this variety. Many students have a preferred area within physics, e.g. electronics, astrophysics or mechanics. However, it is important to remember not to neglect any subject area in its entirety. It is entirely possible that of the four main questions in the ENGAA, several of them could be outside of you comfort zone – leaving you in a very bad position.

Graphs

Graph sketching is usually a tricky area for many students. When tackling a graph sketching problem, there are many approaches however it is useful to start with the basics:

➤ What is the value of y when x is zero?

➤ What is the value of x when y is zero?

➤ Are there any special values of x and y?

➤ If there is a fraction involved, at what values of x is the numerator or denominator equal to zero?

If you asked to draw a function that is the sum, product or division of two (sub) functions, start by drawing out all of the sub functions. Which function is the dominant function when $x > 0$ and $x < 0$.

Answering these basic questions will tell you where the asymptotes and intercepts etc. are, which will help with drawing the function.

Remember the Basics

A surprisingly large number of students do not know what the properties of basic shapes etc. are. For example, the area of a circle is πr^2, the surface area of a sphere is $4\pi r^2$ and the volume of a sphere is $\frac{4}{3}\pi r^3$. To 'go up' a dimension (i.e. to go from an area to a volume) you need to integrate and to 'go down' a dimension you need to differentiate. Learning this will make it easy to remember formulas for the areas and volumes of basic shapes.

It is also important to remember important formulas even though they may be included in formula booklets. The reason for this is that although you may have access to formula booklets during exams, this will not be the case in interviews which will follow the NSAA. In addition, flicking through formula booklets takes up time during an exam and can be avoided if you are able to memorise important formulas.

SECTION 2 Questions

Question 1.1
A golfer swings a club so that the head completes a (virtually) complete circle in T=0.1 s. The length of the club is R=1 m.

What angle from the horizontal should the club hit the ball at to maximise the distance travelled?

[1 mark]

A. 0°

C. 45°

E. Any angle

B. 30°

D. 90°

Question 1.2
What is the (approximate) velocity of the club when it strikes the ball?

[1 mark]

A. 0.1 m/s

C. 10 m/s

E. 100 m/s

B. 3 m/s

D. 60 m/s

Question 1.3
Assuming that the ground is flat, what is the total time the golf ball is in the air?

[3 marks]

A. $3\sqrt{2}$ s

C. $6\sqrt{2}$ s

E. 15 s

B. $5\sqrt{2}$ s

D. 12 s

Question 1.4
What therefore is the maximum horizontal distance the ball travels?

[2 marks]

A. 180 m

C. 360 m

E. 720 m

B. $180\sqrt{2}$ m

D. $360\sqrt{2}$ m

Question 2.1

What is the mass of the moon in terms of the radius of the earth, r, if the density of the Moon is 75% of the density of earth, ρ, and that the radius of the Moon is 4 times smaller than the radius of Earth.

[1 mark]

A. $\frac{1}{64}\rho\pi r^3$

B. $\frac{9}{16}\rho\pi r^3$

C. $\frac{3}{64}\rho\pi r^2$

D. $\frac{3}{64}\rho\pi r^3$

E. $\frac{1}{16}\rho\pi r^3$

Question 2.2

Which of the following is an expression for the acceleration due to gravity on earth, where G is the gravitational constant?

[1 mark]

A. $G\rho\pi r^2$

B. $\frac{3}{4}G\rho\pi r$

C. $\frac{4}{3}G\rho\pi r^2$

D. $\frac{1}{16}G\rho\pi r$

E. $\frac{4}{3}G\rho\pi r$

Question 2.3

Estimate the gravitational acceleration at the surface of the Moon relative to g on earth.

[3 marks]

A. $8g$ B. $\frac{g}{8}$ C. $\frac{g}{16}$ D. $\frac{3g}{16}$ E. $\frac{7g}{16}$

Question 2.4

How would the orbital speed of a satellite of equal mass and equal orbital radius change between orbiting earth and the moon?

[2 marks]

A. Decrease by a factor of $\sqrt{3}/4$
B. Decrease by a factor of 7/16
C. It will be remain unchanged
D. Increase by a factor of 1/16
E. Increase by a factor of 8

Question 3.1

Identical resistors are connected using wire of negligible resistance to a 1.4 V power supply. What would the resistance be of two resistors in parallel?

[1 mark]

A. 2R   B. $\frac{R}{2}$ C. $\frac{3R}{2}$ D. $\frac{2R}{3}$ E. R

Question 3.2

What would the total resistance in this circuit be?

[4 marks]

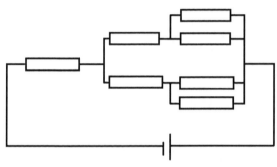

A. 7R   C. $\frac{7R}{3}$ E. $\frac{7R}{4}$

B. 3R

                      D. $\frac{3R}{4}$

Question 3.3

What would R be to produce a total current of 2 A?

[1 mark]

A. 0.01 Ω   D. 0.5 Ω

B. 0.1 Ω   E. 1 Ω

C. 0.2 Ω

Question 3.4

What would be the power dissipated in the circuit?

[1 mark]

A. 0.6 W   C. 2.3 W   E. 3.2 W

B. 1.2 W   D. 2.8 W

Question 4.1
What is Snell's law of reflection?

[1 mark]

A. $\sin\theta_1/\sin\theta_2 = n_2/n_1$

B. $n_1\sin\theta_1 = n_2\sin\theta_2$

C. $n_1/\sin\theta_2 = n_2/\sin\theta_1$

D. $n_1 n_2 = \sin\theta_1 \sin\theta_2$

E. $n_1/\sin\theta_1 = n_2/\sin\theta_2$

Question 4.2
Which of the following is the critical angle of incidence?

[1 mark]

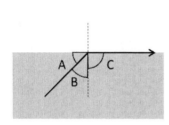 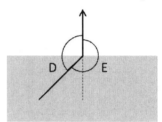

Question 4.3
Carbon disulphide liquid ($n_c = 1.63$) is poured into a container made of crown glass ($n_g = 1.52$). What is the critical angle for internal reflection of a ray in the liquid when it is incident on the liquid-to-glass surface?

[4 marks]

A. 36°   B. 45°   C. 69°   D. 72°   E. 90°

Question 4.4
What is the critical angle of incidence from air to the crown glass?

[1 mark]

A. All light is internally reflected as air is less optically dense than the glass

B. 0°

C. $\arcsin(1/1.52)$

D. 90°

E. There is no critical angle

Question 5.1

A lift with a mass of 800 kg can carry up to 700 kg of passengers. Calculate the total energy needed for an electric motor is used to raise the elevator with a full load from the ground floor to the third floor, 7 m higher. [assume $g=10$ m/s^2]

[1 mark]

A. 105 J   C. 105 kJ   E. 105 MJ
B. 210 J   D. 210 kJ

Question 5.2

Calculate the power of motor required to do this in 30 s.

[1 mark]

A. 700 W   C. 7 kW   E. 70 kW
B. 3500 W   D. 35 kW

Question 5.3

Find the average kinetic energy of the lift and passengers during the ascent.

[2 marks]

A. 41 J   C. 67 J   E. 105 J
B. 52 J   D. 82 J

Question 5.4

The elevator takes 10 s to accelerate and 10 s to decelerate using the same magnitude of constant force in each case. Between acceleration and deceleration no force is used. Calculate the greatest speed which the lift attains.

[3 marks]

A. 0.04 ms^{-1} C. 0.35 ms^{-1} E. 2.3 ms^{-1}
B. 0.14 ms^{-1} D. 1.3 ms^{-1}

Question 6.1

If the friction coefficient between m_1 and m_2 is μ_1 and between m_2 and the inclined plane is μ_2, (where α = the angle of inclination) determine the acceleration of m_2.

[2 marks]

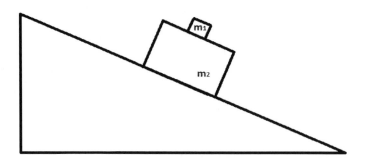

A. $g\,(1 - \mu_2 cos\alpha)$
B. $g\,(\mu_2 sin\alpha - \mu_1 cos\alpha)$
C. $mg\,(sin\alpha - \mu_2 cos\alpha)$
D. $g\,(sin\alpha - \mu_1 cos\alpha)$
E. $g\,(sin\alpha - \mu_2 cos\alpha)$

Question 6.2

Determine the acceleration of m_1 with respect to the plane

[2 marks]

A. $g\,(sin\alpha - \mu_1 cos\alpha)$
B. $mg\,(sin\alpha - \mu_1 cos\alpha)$
C. $g\,sin\alpha\,(\mu_1 - \mu_2)$

D. $g\,(sin\alpha - cos\alpha)$
E. $g\,(\mu_2 sin\alpha - \mu_1 cos\alpha)$

Question 6.3
Determine the acceleration of m_1 with respect to m_2

[2 marks]

A. $g \cos\alpha (\mu_1 + \mu_2)$
B. $g \cos\alpha (\mu_1 - \mu_2)$
C. $g \sin\alpha (\mu_1 - \mu_2)$

D. $mg \cos\alpha (\mu_1 - \mu_2)$
E. $mg \cos\alpha (\mu_1 + \mu_2)$

Question 6.4
Which of the following would give the coefficient of friction?

[1 mark]

A. $\tan(\alpha)$
B. $\cos(\alpha)$

C. $\sin(\alpha)$
D. mg

E. $mg \tan(\alpha)$

Question 7.1
A thin converging lens of focal length $f_1 = 20$ cm is used to produce a magnified image of height 2 cm, 16 cm behind the lens. How far is the 1 cm height object from the lens?

[2 marks]

A. 1 cm
B. 2 cm

C. 5 cm
D. 8 cm

E. 12 cm

Question 7.2
A second thin converging lenses of focal length $f_2 = 10$ cm is placed $d = 30$ cm away. The final image of an object located in front of the first lens is formed 5 cm behind the second lens. Where is the image formed by the first lens?

[3 marks]

A. 5 cm behind the second lens
B. 10 cm behind the second lens
C. 10 cm in front of the second lens
D. 5 cm in front of the second lens
E. 20 cm in front of the second lens

Question 7.3
What is the distance between the original object and the first lens?

[1 mark]

A. 20 cm behind the lens

B. 30 cm behind the lens

C. 40 cm behind the lens

D. 10 cm in front of the lens

E. 25 cm in front of the lens

Question 7.4
Are the images formed real or virtual?

[1 mark]

A. Both virtual

B. Both real

C. First real, second virtual

D. First virtual, second real

E. Cannot be determined

Question 8.1
A sphere of radius R is non-uniformly charged. The density of the charge varies as $\rho(r<R)=ar$ where a is a constant and $\rho(r>R)=0$. What is the charge inside a sphere of radius r<R?

[2 marks]

A. $a\pi r^3$

B. $\frac{4}{3}a\pi r^4$

C. $\frac{4}{3}a\pi r^3$

D. $4a\pi r^4$

E. $a\pi r^4$

Question 8.2
What is the electric potential inside the sphere?

[2 mark]

A. $\dfrac{ar^2}{4\varepsilon}$

B. $\dfrac{a^2 r^2}{4\varepsilon}$

C. $\dfrac{a^2 r}{4\varepsilon}$

D. $\dfrac{aRr}{4\varepsilon}$

E. $\dfrac{aR^2}{4\varepsilon}$

Question 8.3

What is the total charge on the sphere?

[1 mark]

A. $a\pi R^3$

B. $\frac{4}{3}a\pi R^4$

C. $\frac{4}{3}a\pi R^3$

D. $a\pi R^4$

E. $4a\pi R^4$

Question 8.4

How does the magnitude of the electric field outside the sphere changes with the distance r from the centre of the sphere?

[2 marks]

A. $\frac{aR^2}{4\varepsilon r^2}$

B. $\frac{aR^4}{4\varepsilon r^2}$

C. $\frac{aR^4}{4\varepsilon r^3}$

D. $\frac{aR}{4\varepsilon r^3}$

E. $\frac{aR}{4\varepsilon r^2}$

Question 9.1

A ball of mass m is attached to a spring of spring constant k_1 that is itself attached to a spring of spring constant k_2 $(< k_1)$. vWhat is the total spring constant?

[1 mark]

A. k_1+k_2

B. $\sqrt{k_1 + k_2}$

C. $\frac{k_1+k_2}{2}$

D. $\sqrt{\frac{k_1+k_2}{2}}$

E. k_1-k_2

Question 9.2

What is the extension, l_1, of the first spring relative to the second?

[1 mark]

A. l_2 (equal)

B. $k_1 l_2 / k_2$

C. $k_1 / k_2 \, l_2$

D. $k_1 k_2 l_2$

E. $k_2 l_2 / k_1$

Question 9.3

If each of the springs can be extended by length l before breaking, what is the energy of the system?

[3 marks]

A. $(k_1l_1 + k_2l_2)/2$

B. $(k_1l_1^2 + k_2l_2^2)^2$

C. $(k_1l_1^2 + k_2l_2^2)$

D. $(k_1l_1^2 - k_2l_2^2)/2$

E. $(k_1l_1^2 + k_2l_2^2)/2$

Question 9.4

Thus determine the maximum speed of oscillations.

[2 marks]

A. $\frac{(k_1+k_2)l}{m}$

B. $\frac{(k_1+k_2)k_2l}{m}$

C. $\frac{k_2l^2}{k_1m}$

D. $\frac{(k_1+k_2)k_2l^2}{k_1m}$

E. $\frac{(k_1-k_2)k_2l^2}{k_1m}$

Question 10.1

Three point charges $+q$, $+q$ and $-q$ are attached to the vertices of an equilateral triangle of sides a. What is the distance of the centre point from each of the charges?

[1 mark]

A. $\frac{3a}{4}$ B. $\frac{\sqrt{3}a}{4}$ C. $\frac{3a}{2}$ D. $\frac{a}{2}$ E. a

Question 10.2

What is the horizontal component of the field E at the centre point?

[3 marks]

A. $2|E|cos30°$

B. $-|E|cos30°$

C. $|E|cos30°$

D. $|E|sin30°$

E. $E\,0$

Question 10.3

What is the electric field at the centre of the triangle?

[2 marks]

A. $\dfrac{q}{3\pi\epsilon_0 a^2}$

B. $\dfrac{8q}{3\pi\epsilon_0 a^2}$

C. $\dfrac{8q}{\pi\epsilon_0 a^2}$

D. $\dfrac{q}{4\pi\epsilon_0 a}$

E. $\dfrac{3q}{4\pi\epsilon_0 a}$

Question 10.4

What would be the electric field at the centre if all three charges had the same sign?

[1 mark]

A. $\dfrac{q}{4\pi\epsilon_0 a^2}$

B. $\dfrac{-q}{4\pi\epsilon_0 a^2}$

C. $\dfrac{3q}{4\pi\epsilon_0 a^2}$

D. 0

E. None of the above

ANSWERS

Answer Key

Q	A	Q	A	Q	A	Q	A	Q	A	Q	A	Q	A
1	F	31	C	61	D	91	E	121	B	151	D	181	C
2	A	32	G	62	F	92	D	122	A	152	D	182	A
3	D	33	D	63	B	93	A	123	F	153	B	183	E
4	E	34	D	64	A	94	B	124	D	154	E	184	C
5	G	35	E	65	C	95	C	125	A	155	E	185	C
6	C	36	B	66	C	96	D	126	B	156	B	186	A
7	D	37	A	67	G	97	A	127	A	157	C	187	B
8	E	38	E	68	C	98	B	128	F	158	A	188	C
9	D	39	D	69	B	99	C	129	D	159	C	189	B
10	D	40	F	70	B	100	E	130	A	160	B	190	D
11	F	41	E	71	E	101	B	131	D	161	B	191	C
12	B	42	F	72	C	102	C	132	D	162	B	192	C
13	C	43	B	73	E	103	C	133	F	163	C	193	E
14	G	44	C	74	E	104	C	134	B	164	C	194	E
15	D	45	D	75	D	105	E	135	C	165	A	195	A
16	E	46	F	76	E	106	A	136	B	166	C	196	C
17	A	47	E	77	E	107	C	137	C	167	D	197	C
18	E	48	C	78	C	108	E	138	A	168	C	198	E
19	G	49	C	79	E	109	E	139	A	169	D	199	A
20	E	50	B	80	D	110	C	140	C	170	A	200	D
21	H	51	D	81	A	111	E	141	B	171	C	201	C
22	E	52	B	82	B	112	E	142	D	172	B	202	E
23	G	53	G	83	C	113	E	143	C	173	B	203	C
24	D	54	D	84	D	114	B	144	A	174	A	204	D
25	E	55	D	85	B	115	C	145	C	175	C	205	B
26	D	56	A	86	D	116	B	146	C	176	C	206	E
27	G	57	E	87	C	117	B	147	C	177	B	207	A
28	F	58	C	88	E	118	C	148	B	178	A	208	C
29	B	59	D	89	C	119	D	149	D	179	C	209	D
30	A	60	C	90	A	120	C	150	E	180	C	210	E

Section 1: Worked Answers

Question 1: F
That the amplitude of a wave determines its mass is false. Waves are not objects and do not have mass.

Question 2: A
We know that displacement s = 30 m, initial speed u = 0 ms^{-1}, acceleration a = 5.4 ms^{-2}, final speed v = ?, time t = ?
And that $v^2 = u^2 + 2as$
$v^2 = 0 + 2 \times 5.4 \times 30$
$v^2 = 324$ so v = 18 ms^{-1}
and $s = ut + 1/2\ at^2$ so $30 = 1/2 \times 5.4 \times t^2$
$t^2 = 30/2.7$ so t = 3.3 s

Question 3: D
The wavelength is given by: velocity v = λf and frequency f = 1/T so v = λ/T giving wavelength λ = vT
The period T = 49 s/7 so λ = 5 ms^{-1} x 7 s = 35 m

Question 4: E
This is a straightforward question as you only have to put the numbers into the equation (made harder by the numbers being hard to work with).
$$Power = \frac{Force\ x\ Distance}{Time} = \frac{375\ N\ x\ 1.3\ m}{5\ s}$$
$$= 75\ x\ 1.3 = 97.5\ W$$

Question 5: G
v = u + at
v = 0 + 5.6 x 8 = 44.8 ms^{-1}
And $s = ut + \frac{at^2}{2} = 0 + 5.6\ x\frac{8^2}{2} = 179.2$

Question 6: C
The sky diver leaves the plane and will accelerate until the air resistance equals their weight – this is their terminal velocity. The sky diver will accelerate under the force of gravity. If the air resistance force exceeded the force of gravity the sky diver would accelerate away from the ground, and if it was less than the force of gravity they would continue to accelerate toward the ground.

Question 7: D
$s = 20$ m, $u = 0$ ms^{-1}, $a = 10$ ms^{-2}
and $v^2 = u^2 + 2as$
$v^2 = 0 + 2 \times 10 \times 20$
$v^2 = 400$; $v = 20$ ms^{-1}
Momentum = Mass x velocity = $20 \times 0.1 = 2$ kgms^{-1}

Question 8: E
Electromagnetic waves have varying wavelengths and frequencies and their energy is proportional to their frequency.

Question 9: D
The total resistance = $R + r = 0.8 + 1 = 1.8 \, \Omega$
and $I = \dfrac{e.m.f}{total\, resistance} = \dfrac{36}{1.8} = 20\, A$

Question 10: D
Use Newton's second law and remember to work in SI units:
So $Force = mass \times accelaration = mass \times \dfrac{\Delta velocity}{time}$

$= 20 \times 10^{-3} \times \dfrac{100 - 0}{10 \times 10^{-3}}$

$= 200\, N$

Question 11: F

In this case, the work being done is moving the bag 0.7 m

i.e. $Work\ Done\ =\ Bag's\ Weight\ x\ Distance\ =\ 50\ x\ 10\ x\ 0.7 = 350\ N$

$Power = \frac{Work}{Time} = \frac{350}{3} = 116.7\ W$

$= 117$ W to 3 significant figures

Question 12: B

Firstly, use P = Fv to calculate the power [Ignore the frictional force as we are not concerned with the resultant force here].

So P = 300 x 30 = 9000 W

Then, use P = IV to calculate the current.

I = P/V = 9000/200 = 45 A

Question 13: C

Work is defined as W = F x s. Work can also be defined as work = force x distance moved in the direction of force. Work is measured in joules and 1 Joule = 1 Newton x 1 Metre, and 1 Newton = 1 Kg x ms^{-2} [F = ma].

Thus, 1 Joule = Kgm^{2}s^{-2}

Question 14: G

Joules are the unit of energy (and also Work = Force x Distance). Thus, 1 Joule = 1 N x 1 m.

Pa is the unit of Pressure (= Force/Area). Thus, Pa = N x m^{-2}. So J = Nm^{-2} x m^3 = Pa x m^3. Newton's third law describes that every action produces an equal and opposite reaction. For this reason, the energy required to decelerate a body is equal to the amount of energy it possess during movement, i.e. its kinetic energy, which is defined as in statement 1.

Question 15: D

Alpha radiation is of the lower energy, as it represents the movement of a fairly large particle consisting of 2 neutrons and 2 protons. Beta radiation consists of high-energy, high-speed electrons or positrons.

Question 16: E
The half-life does depend on atom type and isotope, as these parameters significantly impact on the physical properties of the atom in general, so statement 1 is false. Statement 2 is the correct definition of half-life. Statement 3 is also correct: half-life in exponential decay will always have the same duration, independent of the quantity of the matter in question; in non-exponential decay, half-life is dependent on the quantity of matter in question.

Question 17: A
In contrast to nuclear fission, where neutrons are shot at unstable atoms, nuclear fusion is based on the high speed, high-temperature collision of molecules, most commonly hydrogen, to form a new, stable atom while releasing energy.

Question 18: E
Nuclear fission releases a significant amount of energy, which is the basis of many nuclear weapons. Shooting neutrons at unstable atoms destabilises the nuclei which in turn leads to a chain reaction and fission. Nuclear fission can lead to the release of ionizing gamma radiation.

Question 19: G
The total resistance of the circuit would be twice the resistance of one resistor and proportional to the voltage, as given by Ohm's Law. Since it is a series circuit, the same current flows through each resistor and since they are identical the potential difference across each resistor will be the same.

Question 20: E
The distance between Earth and Sun = Time x Speed = 60 x 8 seconds x 3 x 10^8 ms^{-1} = 480 x 3 x 10^8 m
Approximately = 1500 x 10^8 = 1.5 x 10^{11} m.
The circumference of Earth's orbit around the sun is given by $2\pi r$ = 2 x 3 x 1.5 x 10^{11}
= 9 x 10^{11} = 10^{12} m

Question 21: H
Speed is a scalar quantity whilst velocity is a vector describing both magnitude and direction. Speed describes the distance a moving object covers over time (i.e. speed = distance/time), whereas velocity describes the rate of change of the displacement of an object (i.e. velocity = displacement/time). The internationally standardised unit for speed is meters per second (ms^{-1}), while ms^{-2} is the unit of acceleration.

Question 22: E
Ohm's Law only applies to conductors and can be mathematically expressed as $V \alpha I$. The easiest way to do this is to write down the equations for statements c, d and e. C: $I \alpha \frac{1}{V}$; D: $I \alpha V^2$; E: $I \alpha V$. Thus, statement E is correct.

Question 23: G
Any object at rest is not accelerating and therefore has no resultant force. Strictly speaking, Newton's second law is actually: Force = rate of change of momentum, which can be mathematically manipulated to give statement 2:

$$Force = \frac{momentum}{time} = \frac{mass \times velocity}{time} = mass \times accelaration$$

Question 24: D

Statement 3 is incorrect, as $Charge = Current \times time$. Statement 1 substitutes $I = \frac{V}{R}$ and statement 2 substitutes $I = \frac{P}{V}$.

Question 25: E
Weight of elevator + people = mg = 10 x (1600 + 200) = 18,000 N
Applying Newton's second law of motion on the car gives:
Thus, the resultant force is given by:
F_M = Motor Force – [Frictional Force + Weight]
F_M = M – 4,000 – 18,000
Use Newton's second law to give: F_M = M – 22,000 N = ma
Thus, M – 22,000 N = 1,800a
Since the lift must accelerate at 1ms^{-2}: M = 1,800 kg x 1 ms^{-2} + 22,000 N
M = 23,800 N

Question 26: D
Total Distance = Distance during acceleration phase + Distance during braking phase
Distance during acceleration phase is given by:
$$s = ut + \frac{at^2}{2} = 0 + \frac{5 \times 10^2}{2} = 250\ m$$
$$v = u + at = 0 + 5 \times 10 = 50\ ms^{-1}$$
And use $a = \frac{v-u}{t}$ to calculate the deceleration: $a = \frac{0-50}{20} = -2.5\ ms^{-2}$
Distance during the deceleration phase is given by:
$$s = ut + \frac{at^2}{2} = 50 \times 20 + \frac{-2.5 \times 20^2}{2} = 1000 - \frac{2.5 \times 400}{2}$$
$$s = 1000 - 500 = 500\ m$$
Thus, $Total\ Distance = 250 + 500 = 750\ m$

Question 27: G
It is not possible to calculate the power of the heater as we don't know the current that flows through it or its internal resistance. The 8 ohms refers to the external copper wire and not the heater. Whilst it's important that you know how to use equations like P = IV, it's more important that you know when you *can't* use them!

Question 28: F
This question has a lot of numbers but not any information on time, which is necessary to calculate power. You cannot calculate power by using P= IV as you don't know how many electrons are accelerated through the potential difference per unit time. Thus, more information is required to calculate the power.

Question 29: B
When an object is in equilibrium with its surroundings, it radiates and absorbs energy at the same rate and so its temperature remains constant i.e. there is no *net* energy transfer. Radiation is slower than conduction and convection.

Question 30: A
The work done by the force is given by:
$$Work\ Done = Force \times Distance = 12\ N \times 3\ m = 36\ J$$

Since the surface is frictionless, $Work\ Done = Kinetic\ Energy$.
$$E_k = \frac{mv^2}{2} = \frac{6v^2}{2}$$
Thus, $36 = 3v^2$
$$v = \sqrt{12} = \sqrt{4}\sqrt{3} = 2\sqrt{3}\ ms^{-1}$$

Question 31: C

$$Total\ energy\ supplied\ to\ water$$
$$= Change\ in\ temperature \times Mass\ of\ water \times 4{,}000\ J$$
$$= 40 \times 1.5 \times 4{,}000 = 240{,}000\ J$$

$$Power\ of\ the\ heater = \frac{Work\ Done}{time} = \frac{240{,}000}{50 \times 60} = \frac{240{,}000}{3{,}000} = 80\ W$$

Using $P = IV = \frac{V^2}{R}$:

$$R = \frac{V^2}{P} = \frac{100^2}{80} = \frac{10{,}000}{80} = 125\ ohms$$

Question 32: G
The large amount of energy released during atomic fission is the basis underlying nuclear power plants. Splitting an atom into two or more parts will by definition produce molecules of different sizes than the original atom; therefore it produces two new atoms. The free neutrons and photons produced by the splitting of atoms form the basis of the energy release.

Question 33: D
Gravitational potential energy is just an extension of the equation work done = force x distance (force is the weight of the object, *mg,* and distance is the height, *h*). The reservoir in statement 3 would have a potential energy of 10^{10} Joules i.e. 10 Giga Joules ($E_p = 10^6$ kg x 10 N x 10^3 m).

Question 34: D
Statement 1 is the common formulation of Newton's third law. Statement 2 presents a consequence of the application of Newton's third law.

Statement 3 is false: rockets can still accelerate because the products of burning fuel are ejected in the opposite direction from which the rocket needs to accelerate.

Question 35: E
Positively charged objects have lost electrons.
$$Charge \ = \ Current \ x \ Time \ = \frac{Voltage}{Resistance} \ x \ Time.$$
Objects can become charged by friction as electrons are transferred from one object to the other.

Question 36: B
Each body of mass exerts a gravitational force on another body with mass. This is true for all planets as well.

Gravitational force is dependent on the mass of both objects. Satellites stay in orbit due to centripetal force that acts tangentially to gravity (not because of the thrust from their engines). Two objects will only land at the same time if they also have the same shape or they are in a vaccum (as otherwise air resistance would result in different terminal velocities).

Question 37: A

Metals conduct electrical charge easily and provide little resistance to the flow of electrons. Charge can also flow in several directions. However, all conductors have an internal resistance and therefore provide *some* resistance to electrical charge.

Question 38: E

First, calculate the rate of petrol consumption:

$$\frac{Speed}{Consumption} = \frac{60 \ miles/hour}{30 \ miles/gallon} = 2 \ gallons/hour$$

Therefore, the total power is:

$2 \ gallons = 2 \ x \ 9 \ x \ 10^8 = 18 \ x \ 10^8 J$

$1 \ hour = 60 \ x \ 60 = 3600 \ s$

$\text{Power} = \frac{Energy}{Time} = \frac{18 \ x 10^8}{3600}$

$P = \frac{18}{36} \ x \ 10^6 = 5 \ x \ 10^5 \ W$

Since efficiency is 20%, the power delivered to the wheels $= 5 \ x \ 10^5 \ x \ 0.2 = 10^5 \ W = 100 \ kW$

Question 39: D

Beta radiation is stopped by a few millimetres of aluminium, but not by paper. In β^- radiation, a neutron changes into a proton plus an emitted electron. This means the atomic mass number remains unchanged.

Question 40: F

Firstly, calculate the mass of the car $= \frac{Weight}{g} = \frac{15,000}{10} = 1,500 \ kg$

Then using $v = u + at$ where v = 0 ms^{-1} and u = 15 ms^{-1} and t = 10 x 10^{-3} s

$a = \frac{0-15}{0.01} = 1500 ms^{-2}$

$F = ma = 1500 \ x \ 1500 = 2 \ 250 \ 000 \ N$

Question 41: E
Electrical insulators offer high resistance to the flow of charge. Insulators are usually non-metals; metals conduct charge very easily. Since charge does not flow easily to even out, they can be charged with friction.

Question 42: A̶ A   'Not true'
The car accelerates for the first 10 seconds at a constant rate and then decelerates after t=30 seconds. It does not reverse, as the velocity is not negative.

Question 43: B
The distance travelled by the car is represented by the area under the curve (integral of velocity) which is given by the area of two triangles and a rectangle:

$$Area = \left(\frac{1}{2} \times 10 \times 10\right) + (20 \times 10) + \left(\frac{1}{2} \times 10 \times 10\right)$$
$$Area = 50 + 200 + 50 = 300\ m$$

Question 44: C
Using the equation force = mass x acceleration, where the unknown acceleration = change in velocity over change in time.

Hence: $\frac{F}{m} = \frac{change\ in\ velocity}{change\ in\ time}$

We know that F = 10,000 N, mass = 1,000 kg and change in time is 5 seconds.

So, $\frac{10,000}{1,000} = \frac{change\ in\ velocity}{5}$

So change in velocity = 10 x 5 = 50 m/s

Question 45: D
This question tests both your ability to convert unusual units into SI units and to select the relevant values (e.g. the crane's mass is not important here).

0.01 tonnes = 10 kg; 100 cm = 1 m; 5,000 ms = 5 s

$$Power = \frac{Work\ Done}{Time} = \frac{Force\ x\ Distance}{Time}$$

In this case the force is the weight of the wardrobe $= 10 \times g = 10 \times 10 = 100N$

Thus, $Power = \frac{100\ x\ 1}{5} = 20\ W$

Question 46: F
Remember that the resistance of a parallel circuit (R_T) is given by: $\frac{1}{R_T} = \frac{1}{R_1} + \frac{1}{R_2} + \ ...$

Thus, $\frac{1}{R_T} = \frac{1}{1} + \frac{1}{2} = \frac{3}{2}$ and therefore $R = \frac{2}{3}\ \Omega$

Using Ohm's Law: $I = \frac{20\ V}{\frac{2}{3}\Omega} = 20 \times \frac{3}{2} = 30\ A$

Question 47: E

Water is denser than air. Therefore, the speed of light decreases when it enters water and increases when it leaves water. The direction of light also changes when light enters/leaves water. This phenomenon is known as refraction and is governed by Snell's Law.

Question 48: C
The voltage in a parallel circuit is the same across each branch, i.e. branch A Voltage = branch B Voltage.
The resistance of Branch A = 6 x 5 = 30 Ω; the resistance of Branch B = 10 x 2 = 20 Ω.
Using Ohm's Law: I= V/R. Thus, $I_A = \frac{60}{30} = 2\ A$; $I_B = \frac{60}{20} = 3\ A$

Question 49: C

This is a very straightforward question made harder by the awkward units you have to work with. Ensure you are able to work comfortably with prefixes of 10^9 and 10^{-9} and convert without difficulty.

50,000,000,000 nano Watts = 50 W and 0.000000004 Giga Amperes = 4 A.

Using $P = IV$: $V = \frac{P}{I} = \frac{50}{4} = 12.5\ V = 0.0125\ kV$

Question 50: B

Radioactive decay is highly random and unpredictable. Only gamma decay releases gamma rays and few types of decay release X-rays. The electrical charge of an atom's nucleus decreases after alpha decay as two protons are lost.

Question 51: D

Using $P = IV$: $I = \frac{P}{V} = \frac{60}{15} = 4\ A$

Now using Ohm's Law: $R = \frac{V}{I} = \frac{15}{4} = 3.75\ \Omega$

So each resistor has a resistance of $\frac{3.75}{3} = 1.25\ \Omega$.

If two more resistors are added, the overall resistance = 1.25 x 5 = 6.25 Ω

Question 52: B

$Total\ Work\ Done\ by\ Engine = Force \times Distance =$

$Weight\ of\ Tractor \times Distance$

Thus, $Work\ Done = 5{,}000 \times 10 \times 100 = 5 \times 10^6 J$

$If\ 1\ ml\ contains\ 20{,}000\ J\ then\ 1{,}000\ ml\ has\ 20{,}000 \times 1{,}000\ J$

$= 2 \times 10^7 J$

$Efficiency = \frac{Useful\ work\ done}{Total\ energy\ used} = \frac{5 \times 10^6}{2 \times 10^7} = 2.5 \times 10^{-1} = 0.25 = 25\%$

Question 53: G

Electromagnetic induction is defined by statements 1 and 2. An electrical current is generated when a coil moves in a magnetic field.

Question 54: D
An ammeter will always give the same reading in a series circuit, not in a parallel circuit where current splits at each branch in accordance with Ohm's Law.

Question 55: D
Electrons move in the opposite direction to current (i.e. they move from negative to positive).

Question 56: A
For a fixed resistor, the current is directly proportional to the potential difference. For a filament lamp, as current increases, the metal filament becomes hotter. This causes the metal atoms to vibrate and move more, resulting in more collisions with the flow of electrons. This makes it harder for the electrons to move through the lamp and results in increased resistance. Therefore, the graph's gradient decreases as current increases.

Question 57: E
Vector quantities consist of both direction and magnitude, e.g. velocity, displacement, etc., and can be added by taking account of direction in the sum.

Question 58: C
The gravity on the moon is 6 times less than 10 ms^{-2}. Thus, g_{moon}= $\frac{10}{6}$ = $\frac{5}{3}$ ms^{-2}.

Since weight = mass x gravity, the mass of the rock = $\frac{250}{\frac{5}{3}}$ = $\frac{750}{5}$ = $150\ kg$

Therefore, the density = $\frac{mass}{volume}$ = $\frac{150}{250}$ = $0.6\ kg/cm^3$

Question 59: D
An alpha particle consists of a helium nucleus. Thus, alpha decay causes the mass number to decrease by 4 and the atomic number to decrease by 2. Five iterations of this would decrease the mass number by 20 and the atomic number by 10.

Question 60: C
Using Ohm's Law: The potential difference entering the transformer (V_1) =

10 x 20 = 200 V

Now use $\frac{N1}{N2} = \frac{V1}{V2}$ to give: $\frac{5}{10} = \frac{200}{V2}$

Thus, $V_2 = \frac{2,000}{5} = 400$ V

Question 61: D
For objects in free fall that have reached terminal velocity, acceleration = 0.
Thus, the sphere's weight = resistive forces.
Using Work Done = Force x Distance: Force = 10,000 J/100 m = 100 N.
Therefore, the sphere's weight = 100 N and since $g = 10ms^{-2}$, the sphere's
mass = 10 kg

Question 62: F
The wave length of ultraviolet waves is longer than that of x-rays.
Wavelength is inversely proportional to frequency. Most electromagnetic
waves are not stopped with aluminium (and require thick lead to stop them),
and they travel at the speed of light. Humans can only see a very small part
of the spectrum.

Question 63: B
If an object moves towards the sensor, the wavelength will appear to
decrease and the frequency increase. The faster this happens, the faster the
increase in frequency and decrease in wavelength.

Question 64: A
$Acceleration = \frac{Change\ in\ Velocity}{Time} = \frac{1,000}{0.1} = 10,000\ ms^{-2}$

Using Newton's second law: The Braking Force = Mass x Acceleration.

Thus, Braking Force = 10,000 x 0.005 = $50\ N$

Question 65: C
Polonium has undergone alpha decay. Thus, Y is a helium nucleus and contains 2 protons and 2 neutrons.
Therefore, 10 moles of Y contain 2 x 10 x 6 x 10^{23} protons = 120 x 10^{23} = 1.2 x 10^{25} protons.

Question 66: C
The rod's activity is less than 1,000 Bq after 300 days. In order to calculate the longest possible half-life, we must assume that the activity is just below 1,000 Bq after 300 days. Thus, the half-life has decreased activity from 16,000 Bq to 1,000 Bq in 300 days.
After one half-life: Activity = 8,000 Bq
After two half-lives: Activity = 4,000 Bq
After three half-lives: Activity = 2,000 Bq
After four half-lives: Activity = 1,000 Bq
Thus, the rod has halved its activity a minimum of 4 times in 300 days.
300/4 = 75 days

Question 67: G

There is no change in the atomic mass or proton numbers in gamma radiation. In β decay, a neutron is transformed into a proton (and an electron is released). This results in an increase in proton number by 1 but no overall change in atomic mass. Thus, after 5 rounds of beta decay, the proton number will be 89 + 5 = 94 and the mass number will remain at 200. Therefore, there are 94 protons and 200-94 = 106 neutrons.
NB: You are not expected to know about β^+ decay.

Question 68: C
Calculate the speed of the sound $= \dfrac{distance}{time} = \dfrac{500}{1.5} = 333 \ ms^{-1}$

Thus, the $Wavelength = \dfrac{Speed}{Frequency} = \dfrac{333}{440}$

Approximate 333 to 330 to give: $\dfrac{330}{440} = \dfrac{3}{4} = 0.75 \ m$

Question 69: B
Firstly, note the all the answer options are a magnitude of 10 apart. Thus, you don't have to worry about getting the correct numbers as long as you get the correct power of 10. You can therefore make your life easier by rounding, e.g. approximate π to 3, etc.

The area of the shell $= \pi r^2$.

$= \pi \times (50 \times 10^{-3})^2 = \pi \times (5 \times 10^{-2})^2$

$= \pi \times 25 \times 10^{-4} = 7.5 \times 10^{-3} \, m^2$

The deceleration of the shell $= \frac{u-v}{t} = \frac{200}{500 \times 10^{-6}} = 0.4 \times 10^6 \, ms^{-2}$

Then, using Newton's Second Law:

$Braking\ force = mass \times acceleration = 1 \times 0.4 \times 10^6 = 4 \times 10^5 N$

Finally: $Pressure = \frac{Force}{Area} = \frac{4 \times 10^5}{7.5 \times 10^{-3}} = \frac{8}{15} \times 10^8 \, Pa \approx 5 \times 10^7 Pa$

Question 70: B
The fountain transfers 10% of 1,000 J of energy per second into 120 litres of water per minute. Thus, it transfers 100 J into 2 litres of water per second.

Therefore the Total Gravitational Potential Energy, $E_p = mg\Delta h$

Thus, $100 \, J = 2 \times 10 \times h$

Hence, $h = \frac{100}{20} = 5 \, m$

Question 71: E
In step down transformers, the number of turns of the primary coil is larger than that of the secondary coil to decrease the voltage. If a transformer is 100% efficient, the electrical power input = electrical power output (P=IV).

Question 72: C
The percentage of C^{14} in the bone halves every 5,730 years. Since it has decreased from 100% to 6.25%, it has undergone 4 half-lives. Thus, the bone is 4 x 5,730 years old = 22,920 years

Question 73: E

This is a straightforward question in principle, as it just requires you to plug the values into the equation: $Velocity = Wavelength \times Frequency$ – Just ensure you work in SI units to get the correct answer.

$$Frequency = \frac{2\ m/s}{2.5\ m} = 0.8\ Hz = 0.8 \times 10^{-6} MHz = 8 \times 10^{-7}\ MHz$$

Question 74: E

If an element has a half-life of 25 days, its BQ value will be halved every 25 days.

A total of 350/25 = 14 half-lives have elapsed. Thus, the count rate has halved 14 times. Therefore, to calculate the original rate, the final count rate must be doubled 14 times = 50×2^{14}.

$2^{14} = 2^5 \times 2^5 \times 2^4 = 32 \times 32 \times 16 = 16{,}384$.

Therefore, the original count rate = 16,384 x 50 = 819,200

Question 75: D

Remember that $V = IR = \frac{P}{I}$ and

$$Power = \frac{Work\ Done}{Time} = \frac{Force\ x\ Distance}{Time} = Force\ x\ Velocity;$$

Thus, A is derived from: $V = IR$,

B is derived from: $= \frac{P}{I}$,

C is derived from: $Voltage = \frac{Power}{Current} = \frac{Force\ x\ Velocity}{Current}$,

Since $Charge = Current\ x\ Time$, E and F are derived from: $Voltage =$

$$\frac{Power}{Current} = \frac{Force\ x\ Distance}{Time\ x\ Current} = \frac{J}{As} = \frac{J}{C},$$

D is incorrect as Nm = J. Thus the correct variant would be NmC^{-1}

Question 76: E

Forces on the ball are $weight = mg$ which is constant and tension T which varies with position.

$$F = ma\,;\ a = \frac{v^2}{r}$$

$$T + mg = m\frac{v^2}{r}$$

If the ball stops moving in a circle it means there is no tension in the string

(T=0) so: $mg = m\frac{v^2}{r}$

$$v = \sqrt{gr}$$

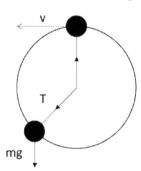

Question 77: E

To move at a steady velocity there is no acceleration so the forces are balanced. Resolve along the slope: $F + mg\sin(30) = T\cos(30)$

$$\frac{mg}{2} + F = \frac{T\sqrt{3}}{2}$$

$$T = \frac{2}{\sqrt{3}}\left(\frac{mg}{2} + F\right)$$

Work done in pulling the box W=Fd so: $P = vT\cos(30)$

$$P = \left(\frac{mg}{2} + F\right)v$$

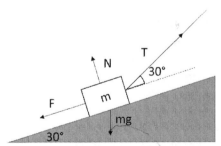

Question 78: C

This is a conservation of energy problem. In the absence of friction there is no dissipation of energy therefore the sum of the potential and kinetic energy must be constant: $\frac{1}{2}mv^2 + mgh = E$

At its highest the velocity and kinetic energy are 0 so $E = mgh_1$.

At the bottom of the swing the potential energy at h is converted to kinetic energy.

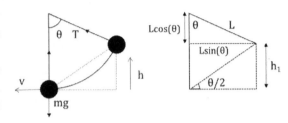

Therefore: $\frac{1}{2}mv^2 = E = mgh_1 \therefore v = \sqrt{2gh_1}$

$h_1 = l(1 - \cos(\theta))$

$v = \sqrt{2gh_1} = \sqrt{2gl(1 - \cos(\theta))}$

Question 79: E

Conservation of momentum. Before : $p = mu_1$

Afterward: $p = m(v_1 + v_2)$

Vertical components must cancel therefore: $v_2 \sin(\theta) = 2v_2 \sin(30°)$

$\sin(\theta) = 1$ giving $\theta = 90°$

Question 80: D

Elastic collision means kinetic energy is conserved so three balls will swing at a velocity equal to the velocity of the first to conserve both momentum and kinetic energy.

$$\frac{1}{2}mv^2 = \frac{1}{2}m_2u^2$$

But momentum is also conserved so $mv = m_2u$

Mass must therefore be equal i.e. 3 balls move at a velocity $u = v$

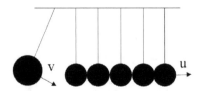

Question 81: A

The ball will follow a parabolic trajectory. The minimum angle is therefore given by the gradient of the parabola which goes through the points (0,3) and (-6,0). [**NB:** do not use a triangle, the ball has weight]

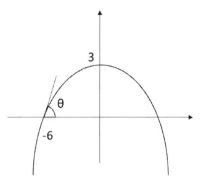

$$y = -ax^2 + 3$$
$$0 = -36a + 3$$
$$a = \frac{1}{6}$$
$$y = -\frac{x^2}{6} + 3$$
$$\frac{dy}{dx} = -\frac{x}{3}$$
$$\frac{dy}{dx} = -\frac{6}{3} = -2 \quad \therefore \tan(\theta) = -2 = 2$$
$$\theta = \arctan(2)$$

Question 82: B

Simple harmonic motion $m\frac{d^2x}{dt^2} = -kx$

Hence: $T \propto \sqrt{\frac{m}{k}}$.

Doubling k and halving m would therefore reduce time period T by a half. The frequency is the reciprocal of the time period and will therefore double.

Question 83: C

At the top of the bounce the kinetic energy is zero as velocity is zero. Highest velocity will be downwards before impact where *potential energy lost = kinetic energy gained* (assuming no resistance).

$$\frac{1}{2}mv^2 = mgh$$
$$v^2 = 2gh = 60$$
$$v = 2\sqrt{15}$$

Question 84: D

Speed is close to c so need to consider Lorentz contraction in special relativity: $l' = l\sqrt{1 - \frac{v^2}{c^2}}$

$$= l\sqrt{1 - \frac{\left(\frac{c}{10}\right)^2}{c^2}}$$

$$= l\sqrt{0.99}$$

Question 85: B

Initial kinetic energy must equal work done to stop the car: $\frac{1}{2}mv^2 = Fd = \frac{mg}{2}d$

$$v^2 = gd$$

$$d = \frac{v^2}{g}$$

Question 86: D

Find the proportion of amplitude left, then use this to work out how many half-lives have passed: $\frac{25}{200} = \frac{1}{8} = \frac{1}{2^3}$

Therefore 12 seconds is three half-lives and t=4s.

Question 87: C

$$f_{beats} = |f_1 - f_2| = \frac{1}{8}f = 10$$

$$f = 80 \text{ Hz}$$

Question 88: E

The two waves would interfere destructively as they are half a wavelength phase difference. A wave would reflect back onto itself in this way if reflected in a plane, perpendicular surface. These two waves travelling in opposite directions (incident and reflected) would produce a standing wave, with this exact point in time corresponding to zero amplitude. There are 5 nodes with two fixed ends making it the 4th harmonic of a standing wave. Thus, all the statements are true.

Question 89: C

Beta decay changes a neutron to a proton releasing an electron and an antineutrino (a doesn't change, b increases by one), then alpha decay emits an alpha particle which is two protons and two neutron (a decreases by 4, b decreases by two).

Question 90: A

Assume ideal gas: $PV = nRT$

$$P_2 = \frac{nR2T}{1.1V}$$

Therefore change in P is equal to $\frac{2}{1.1} = 1.818$ which is an 82% increase.

Question 91: E

Alpha particles are +2 and are deflected to the right. Were they a -1 charge they would follow path Q however electrons have a far smaller mass and will be deflected much more than an alpha particle.

Question 92: D

Assume brightness increases with current. Work out total resistance, then total current and then split between resistors within the circuit.

For three in parallel: $\frac{1}{R_T} = \sum \frac{1}{R} = \frac{3}{R}$ $\therefore$ $R_T = \frac{R}{3}$

$$I_T = \frac{V}{R_T} = \frac{3V}{R}$$

Therefore, current in each lamp is one third of this (split equally as equal resistance in each branch): $I_{1,2,3} = \frac{V}{R}$

For two in series and one in parallel, the two in series have resistance 2R so:

$\frac{1}{R_T} = \frac{1}{2R} + \frac{1}{R}$ $\therefore$ $R_T = \frac{2R}{3}$

$$I_T = \frac{V}{R_T} = \frac{3V}{2R}$$

This is split with a third going to the branch with resistance 2R and two thirds going to the branch with resistance R: $I_6 = \frac{V}{R}$; $I_{4,5} = \frac{V}{2R}$

In series the total resistance is simple 3R so: $I_T = \frac{V}{R_T} = \frac{V}{3R}$

Current is equal in all and is equal to the total current so: $I_{7,8,9} = \frac{V}{3R}$

Current in 1,2,3 and 4 is the same and is greatest.

Question 93: A

Object is between f and the
lens so rays will diverge on
the other side producing a
virtual image on the same
side which is magnified.

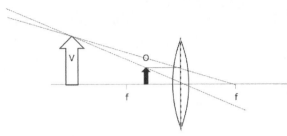

Question 94: B

Moments taken with the pivot at the wall must balance therefore:

$$\frac{2}{3} lT \sin \theta = lmg$$

$$T = \frac{3mg}{2 \sin \theta}$$

Question 95: C

This process is known as the photoelectric effect (photons producing
electron emission) and the presence of a work function arises due to wave
particle duality. [n.b. thermionic emission uses heat not incident radiation to
emit particles]. As the axis is kinetic energy and not potential, the intercept
is the work function not the stopping potential.

Question 96: D

Huygens' principle states that every point on a wavefront is like a point
source of a wave travelling at the same speed. This explains the first four
but does not account for energy loss during propagation i.e. damping.

Question 97: A

Carnot cycle is the most efficient where: $\eta = \frac{work\ done}{heat\ put\ in} = 1 - \frac{T_{cold}}{T_{hot}} = 1 -$

$\frac{280}{420} = \frac{3}{7} \approx 43\%$

Question 98: B
B is the only correct statement. NB- while generators can have a moving coil, they could equally have a moving magnetic field instead so this is not true.

Question 99: C
NAND (gives X), OR (gives Y) and AND (gives Z) gates

Question 100: E
Several almost synonymous terms. Those in bold are correct. E is the only line with all three.

	P	Q	R
A	**Elastic Modulus**	**Yield stress**	Fracture toughness
B	**Tensile Modulus**	**Plastic onset**	Yield stress
C	Hardness	**Stiffness**	**Ductile failure**
D	Ductility	**Elastic limit**	Brittle fracture
E	**Young's Modulus**	**Yield stress**	**Fracture stress**

Question 101: B

Each three-block combination is mutually exclusive to any other combination, so the probabilities are added. Each block pick is independent of all other picks, so the probabilities can be multiplied. For this scenario there are three possible combinations:

P(2 red blocks and 1 yellow block) = P(red then red then yellow) + P(red then yellow then red) + P(yellow then red then red) =

$(\frac{12}{20} \times \frac{11}{19} \times \frac{8}{18}) + (\frac{12}{20} \times \frac{8}{19} \times \frac{11}{18}) + (\frac{8}{20} \times \frac{12}{19} \times \frac{11}{18}) =$

$\frac{3 \times 12 \times 11 \times 8}{20 \times 19 \times 18} = \frac{44}{95}$

Question 102: C

Multiply through by 15: $3(3x + 5) + 5(2x - 2) = 18 \times 15$

Thus: $9x + 15 + 10x - 10 = 270$

$9x + 10x = 270 - 15 + 10$

$19x = 265$

$x = 13.95$

Question 103: C

This is a rare case where you need to factorise a complex polynomial:

$(3x\ )(x\ ) = 0$, possible pairs: 2 x 10, 10 x 2, 4 x 5, 5 x 4

$(3x - 4)(x + 5) = 0$

$3x - 4 = 0$, so $x = \frac{4}{3}$

$x + 5 = 0$, so $x = -5$

Question 104: C

$\dfrac{5(x-4)}{(x+2)(x-4)} + \dfrac{3(x+2)}{(x+2)(x-4)}$

$= \dfrac{5x-20+3x+6}{(x+2)(x-4)}$

$= \dfrac{8x-14}{(x+2)(x-4)}$

Question 105: E

$p \propto \sqrt[3]{q}$, so $p = k \sqrt[3]{q}$

$p = 12$ when $q = 27$ gives $12 = k \sqrt[3]{27}$, so $12 = 3k$ and $k = 4$

so $p = 4 \sqrt[3]{q}$

Now $p = 24$:

$24 = 4\sqrt[3]{q}$, so $6 = \sqrt[3]{q}$ and $q = 6^3 = 216$

Question 106: A

$8 \times 9 = 72$

$8 = (4 \times 2) = 2 \times 2 \times 2$

$9 = 3 \times 3$

$(2 \times 2 \times 2 \times 3 \times 3)^2 = 2 \times 2 \times 2 \times 2 \times 2 \times 2 \times 3 \times 3 \times 3 \times 3 = 2^6 \times 3^4$

Question 107: C

Note that $1.151 \times 2 = 2.302$.

Thus: $\dfrac{2 \times 10^5 + 2 \times 10^2}{10^{10}} = 2 \times 10^{-5} + 2 \times 10^{-8}$

$= 0.00002 + 0.00000002 = 0.00002002$

Question 108: E

$y^2 + ay + b$

$= (y + 2)^2 - 5 = y^2 + 4y + 4 - 5$

$= y^2 + 4y + 4 - 5 = y^2 + 4y - 1$

So $a = 4$ and $y = -1$

Question 109: E

Take $5(m + 4n)$ as a common factor to give: $\frac{4(m+4n)}{5(m+4n)} + \frac{5(m-2n)}{5(m+4n)}$

Simplify to give: $\frac{4m+16n+5m-10n}{5(m+4n)} = \frac{9m+6n}{5(m+4n)} = \frac{3(3m+2n)}{5(m+4n)}$

Question 110: C

$A \propto \frac{1}{\sqrt{B}}$. Thus, $= \frac{k}{\sqrt{B}}$.

Substitute the values in to give: $4 = \frac{k}{\sqrt{25}}$.

Thus, $k = 20$.

Therefore, $A = \frac{20}{\sqrt{B}}$.

When B = 16, $A = \frac{20}{\sqrt{16}} = \frac{20}{4} = 5$

Question 111: E

Angles SVU and STU are opposites and add up to 180°, so STU = 91°

The angle of the centre of a circle is twice the angle at the circumference so

SOU = 2 x 91° = 182°

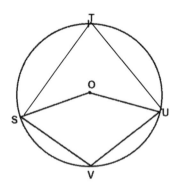

Question 112: E

The surface area of an open cylinder $A = 2\pi rh$. Cylinder B is an enlargement of A, so the increases in radius (r) and height (h) will be proportional: $\frac{r_A}{r_B} = \frac{h_A}{h_B}$. Let us call the proportion coefficient n, where n = $\frac{r_A}{r_B} = \frac{h_A}{h_B}$.

So $\frac{Area\ A}{Area\ B} = \frac{2\pi r_A h_A}{2\pi r_B h_B} = n \times n = n^2$. $\frac{Area\ A}{Area\ B} = \frac{32\pi}{8\pi} = 4$, so n = 2.

The proportion coefficient n = 2 also applies to their volumes, where the third dimension (also radius, i.e. the r^2 in $V = \pi r^2 h$) is equally subject to this constant of proportionality. The cylinder's volumes are related by $n^3 = 8$.

If the smaller cylinder has volume 2π cm^3, then the larger will have volume $2\pi \times n^3 = 2\pi \times 8 = 16\pi$ cm^3.

Question 113: E

$$= \frac{8}{x(3-x)} - \frac{6(3-x)}{x(3-x)}$$

$$= \frac{8 - 18 + 6x}{x(3-x)}$$

$$= \frac{6x - 10}{x(3-x)}$$

Question 114: B

For the black ball to be drawn in the last round, white balls must be drawn every round. Thus the probability is given by

$$P = \frac{9}{10} \times \frac{8}{9} \times \frac{7}{8} \times \frac{6}{7} \times \frac{5}{6} \times \frac{4}{5} \times \frac{3}{4} \times \frac{2}{3} \times \frac{1}{2}$$

$$= \frac{9 \times 8 \times 7 \times 6 \times 5 \times 4 \times 3 \times 2 \times 1}{10 \times 9 \times 8 \times 7 \times 6 \times 5 \times 4 \times 3 \times 2 \times 1} = \frac{1}{10}$$

Question 115: C

The probability of getting a king the first time is $\frac{4}{52} = \frac{1}{13}$, and the probability of getting a king the second time is $\frac{3}{51}$. These are independent events, thus, the probability of drawing two kings is $\frac{1}{13} x \frac{3}{51} = \frac{3}{663} = \frac{1}{221}$

Question 116: B

The probabilities of all outcomes must sum to one, so if the probability of rolling a 1 is x, then: $x + x + x + x + 2x = 1$. Therefore, $x = \frac{1}{7}$.

The probability of obtaining two sixes $P_{12} = \frac{2}{7} x \frac{2}{7} = \frac{4}{49}$

Question 117: B

There are plenty of ways of counting, however the easiest is as follows: 0 is divisible by both 2 and 3. Half of the numbers from 1 to 36 are even (i.e. 18 of them). 3, 9, 15, 21, 27, 33 are the only numbers divisible by 3 that we've missed. There are 25 outcomes divisible by 2 or 3, out of 37.

Question 118: C

List the six ways of achieving this outcome: HHTT, HTHT, HTTH, and TTHH, THTH, THHT. There are 2^4 possible outcomes for 4 consecutive coin flips, so the probability of two heads and two tails is: $6 x \frac{1}{2^4} = \frac{6}{16} = \frac{5}{8}$

Question 119: D

Count the number of ways to get a 5, 6 or 7 (draw the square if helpful). The ways to get a 5 are: 1, 4; 2, 3; 3, 2; 4, 1. The ways to get a 6 are: 1, 5; 2, 4; 3, 3; 4, 2; 5, 1. The ways to get a 7 are: 1, 6; 2, 5; 3, 4; 4, 3; 5, 2; 6, 1. That is 15 out of 36 possible outcomes.

	1	2	3	4	5	6
1	2	3	4	5	6	7
2	3	4	5	6	7	8
3	4	5	6	7	8	9
4	5	6	7	8	9	10
5	6	7	8	9	10	11
6	7	8	9	10	11	12

Question 120: C

There are x+y+z balls in the bag, and the probability of picking a red ball is $\frac{x}{(x+y+z)}$ and the probability of picking a green ball is $\frac{z}{(x+y+z)}$. These are independent events, so the probability of picking red then green is $\frac{xz}{(x+y+z)^2}$ and the probability of picking green then red is the same. These outcomes are mutually exclusive, so are added.

Question 121: B

There are two ways of doing it, pulling out a red ball then a blue ball, or pulling out a blue ball and then a red ball. Let us work out the probability of the first: $\frac{x}{(x+y+z)} \times \frac{y}{x+y+z-1}$, and the probability of the second option will be the same. These are mutually exclusive options, so the probabilities may be summed.

Question 122: A

[x: Player 1 wins point, y: Player 2 wins point]

Player 1 wins in five rounds if we get: yxxxx, xyxxx, xxyxx, xxxyx.

(Note the case of xxxxy would lead to player 1 winning in 4 rounds, which the question forbids.)

Each of these have a probability of $p^4(1\text{-}p)$. Thus, the solution is $4p^4(1\text{-}p)$.

Question 123: F

$4x + 7 + 18x + 20 = 14$

$22x + 27 = 14$

Thus, $22x = -13$

Giving $x = -\frac{13}{22}$

Question 124: D

$r^3 = \dfrac{3V}{4\pi}$

Thus, $r = \left(\dfrac{3V}{4\pi}\right)^{1/3}$

Therefore, $S = 4\pi\left[\left(\dfrac{3V}{4\pi}\right)^{\frac{1}{3}}\right]^2 = 4\pi\left(\dfrac{3V}{4\pi}\right)^{\frac{2}{3}}$

$= \dfrac{4\pi(3V)^{\frac{2}{3}}}{(4\pi)^{\frac{2}{3}}} = (3V)^{\frac{2}{3}} \times \dfrac{(4\pi)^1}{(4\pi)^{\frac{2}{3}}}$

$= (3V)^{\frac{2}{3}}(4\pi)^{1-\frac{2}{3}} = (4\pi)^{\frac{1}{3}}(3V)^{\frac{2}{3}}$

Question 125: A

Let each unit length be x.

Thus, $S = 6x^2$. Therefore, $x = \left(\frac{S}{6}\right)^{\frac{1}{2}}$

$V = x^3$. Thus, $V = [\left(\frac{S}{6}\right)^{\frac{1}{2}}]^3$ so $V = \left(\frac{S}{6}\right)^{\frac{3}{2}}$

Question 126: B

Multiplying the second equation by 2 we get 4x + 16y = 24. Subtracting the first equation from this we get 13y = 17, so y = $\frac{17}{13}$. Then solving for x we get x = $\frac{10}{13}$. You could also try substituting possible solutions one by one, although given that the equations are both linear and contain easy numbers, it is quicker to solve them algebraically.

Question 127: A

Multiply by the denominator to give: $(7x + 10) = (3y^2 + 2)(9x + 5)$

Partially expand brackets on right side: $(7x + 10) = 9x(3y^2 + 2) + 5(3y^2 + 2)$

Take x terms across to left side: $7x - 9x(3y^2 + 2) = 5(3y^2 + 2) - 10$

Take x outside the brackets: $x[7 - 9(3y^2 + 2)] = 5(3y^2 + 2) - 10$

Thus: $x = \frac{5(3y^2 + 2) - 10}{7 - 9(3y^2 + 2)}$

Simplify to give: $x = \frac{(15y^2)}{(7 - 9(3y^2 + 2))}$

Question 128: F

$$3x \left(\frac{3x^7}{x^{\frac{1}{3}}} \right)^3 = 3x \left(\frac{3^3 x^{21}}{x^{\frac{3}{3}}} \right)$$

$$= 3x \frac{27x^{21}}{x} = 81x^{21}$$

Question 129: D

$$2x[2^{\frac{7}{14}} x^{\frac{7}{14}}] = 2x[2^{\frac{1}{2}} x^{\frac{1}{2}}]$$

$$= 2x(\sqrt{2} \sqrt{x}) = 2 \left[\sqrt{x}\sqrt{x} \right]\left[\sqrt{2} \sqrt{x} \right]$$

$$= 2\sqrt{2x^3}$$

Question 130: A

$A = \pi r^2$, therefore $10\pi = \pi r^2$

Thus, $r = \sqrt{10}$

Therefore, the circumference is $2\pi\sqrt{10}$

Question 131: D

$3.4 = 12 + (3 + 4) = 19$

$19.5 = 95 + (19 + 5) = 119$

Question 132: D

$$2.3 = \frac{2^3}{2} = 4$$

$$4.2 = \frac{4^2}{4} = 4$$

Question 133: F

This is a tricky question that requires you to know how to 'complete the square':

$(x + 1.5)(x + 1.5) = x^2 + 3x + 2.25$

Thus, $(x + 1.5)^2 - 7.25 = x^2 + 3x - 5 = 0$

Therefore, $(x + 1.5)^2 = 7.25 = \frac{29}{4}$

Thus, $x + 1.5 = \sqrt{\frac{29}{4}}$

Thus $x = -\frac{3}{2} \pm \sqrt{\frac{29}{4}} = -\frac{3}{2} \pm \frac{\sqrt{29}}{2}$

Question 134: B

Whilst you definitely need to solve this graphically, it is necessary to complete the square for the first equation to allow you to draw it more easily:

$(x + 2)^2 = x^2 + 4x + 4$

Thus, $y = (x + 2)^2 + 10 = x^2 + 4x + 14$

This is now an easy curve to draw ($y = x^2$ that has moved 2 units left and 10 units up). The turning point of this quadratic is to the left and well above anything in x^3, so the only solution is the first intersection of the two curves in the upper right quadrant around (3.4, 39).

Question 135: C

By far the easiest way to solve this is to sketch them (don't waste time solving them algebraically). As soon as you've done this, it'll be very obvious that $y = 2$ and $y = 1-x^2$ don't intersect, since the latter has its turning point at $(0, 1)$ and zero points at $x = -1$ and 1. $y = x$ and $y = x^2$ intersect at the origin and $(1, 1)$, and $y = 2$ runs through both.

Question 136: B

Notice that you're not required to get the actual values – just the number's magnitude. Thus, 897653 can be approximated to 900,000 and 0.009764 to 0.01. Therefore, 900,000 x 0.01 = 9,000

Question 137: C

Multiply through by 70: $7(7x + 3) + 10(3x + 1) = 14 \times 70$
Simplify: $49x + 21 + 30x + 10 = 980$
$79x + 31 = 980$
$x = \dfrac{949}{79}$

Question 138: A

Split the equilateral triangle into 2 right-angled triangles and apply Pythagoras' theorem:

$x^2 = \left(\frac{x}{2}\right)^2 + h^2$. Thus $h^2 = \frac{3}{4}x^2$

$h = \sqrt{\frac{3x^2}{4}} = \frac{\sqrt{3x^2}}{2}$

The area of a triangle = ½ x base x height $= \frac{1}{2}x\frac{\sqrt{3x^2}}{2}$

Simplifying gives: $x\frac{\sqrt{3x^2}}{4} = x\frac{\sqrt{3}\sqrt{x^2}}{4} = \frac{x^2\sqrt{3}}{4}$

Question 139: A

This is a question testing your ability to spot 'the difference between two squares'.

Factorise to give: $3 - \frac{7x(5x-1)(5x+1)}{(7x)^2(5x+1)}$

Cancel out: $3 - \frac{(5x-1)}{7x}$

Question 140: C

The easiest way to do this is to 'complete the square':

$(x-5)^2 = x^2 - 10x + 25$

Thus, $(x-5)^2 - 125 = x^2 - 10x - 100 = 0$

Therefore, $(x-5)^2 = 125$

$x - 5 = \pm\sqrt{125} = \pm\sqrt{25}\sqrt{5} = \pm5\sqrt{5}$

$x = 5 \pm 5\sqrt{5}$

Question 141: B

Factorise by completing the square:

$x^2 - 4x + 7 = (x - 2)^2 + 3$

Simplify: $(x - 2)^2 = y^3 + 2 - 3$

$x - 2 = \pm\sqrt{y^3 - 1}$

$x = 2 \pm \sqrt{y^3 - 1}$

Question 142: D

Square both sides to give: $(3x + 2)^2 = 7x^2 + 2x + y$

Thus: $y = (3x + 2)^2 - 7x^2 - 2x = (9x^2 + 12x + 4) - 7x^2 - 2x$

$y = 2x^2 + 10x + 4$

Question 143: C

This is a fourth order polynomial, which you aren't expected to be able to factorise at GCSE. This is where looking at the options makes your life a lot easier. In all of them, opening the bracket on the right side involves making $(y \pm 1)^4$ on the left side, i.e. the answers are hinting that $(y \pm 1)^4$ is the solution to the fourth order polynomial.

Since there are negative terms in the equations (e.g. $- 4y^3$), the solution has to be:

$(y - 1)^4 = y^4 - 4y^3 + 6y^2 - 4y + 1$

Therefore, $(y - 1)^4 + 1 = x^5 + 7$

Thus, $y - 1 = (x^5 + 6)^{\frac{1}{4}}$

$y = 1 + (x^5 + 6)^{1/4}$

Question 144: A

Let the width of the television be 4x and the height of the television be 3x.

Then by Pythagoras: $(4x)^2 + (3x)^2 = 50^2$

Simplify: $25x^2 = 2500$

Thus: $x = 10$. Therefore: the screen is 30 inches by 40 inches, i.e. the area is 1,200 inches^2.

Question 145: C

Square both sides to give: $1 + \frac{3}{x^2} = (y^5 + 1)^2$

Multiply out: $\frac{3}{x^2} = (y^{10} + 2y^5 + 1) - 1$

Thus: $x^2 = \frac{3}{y^{10}+2y^5}$

Therefore: $x = \sqrt{\frac{3}{y^{10} + 2y^5}}$

Question 146: C

The easiest way is to double the first equation and triple the second to get:

$6x - 10y = 20 \ and \ 6x + 6y = 39$.

Subtract the first from the second to give: $16y = 19$,

Therefore, $y = \frac{19}{16}$.

Substitute back into the first equation to give $x = \frac{85}{16}$.

Question 147: C

This is fairly straightforward; the first inequality is the easier one to work with: B and D and E violate it, so we just need to check A and C in the second inequality.

C: $1^3 - 2^2 < 3$, but A: $2^3 - 1^2 > 3$

Question 148: B

Whilst this can be done graphically, it's quicker to do algebraically (because the second equation is not as easy to sketch). Intersections occur where the curves have the same coordinates.

Thus: $x + 4 = 4x^2 + 5x + 5$

Simplify: $4x^2 + 4x + 1 = 0$

Factorise: $(2x + 1)(2x + 1) = 0$

Thus, the two graphs only intersect once at $x = -\frac{1}{2}$

Question 149: D

It's better to do this algebraically as the equations are easy to work with and you would need to sketch very accurately to get the answer. Intersections occur where the curves have the same coordinates. Thus: $x^3 = x$

$x^3 - x = 0$

Thus: $x(x^2 - 1) = 0$

Spot the 'difference between two squares': $x(x + 1)(x - 1) = 0$

Thus there are 3 intersections: at $x = 0, 1 \ and -1$

Question 150: E

Note that the line is the hypotenuse of a right angled triangle with one side unit length and one side of length ½. By Pythagoras, $\left(\frac{1}{2}\right)^2 + 1^2 = x^2$

Thus, $x^2 = \frac{1}{4} + 1 = \frac{5}{4}$

$$x = \sqrt{\frac{5}{4}} = \frac{\sqrt{5}}{\sqrt{4}} = \frac{\sqrt{5}}{2}$$

Question 151: D

We can eliminate z from equation (1) and (2) by multiplying equation (1) by 3 and adding it to equation (2):

$3x + 3y - 3z = -3$ Equation (1) multiplied by 3

$\underline{2x - 2y + 3z = 8}$ Equation (2) then add both equations

$5x + y \quad\quad = 5$ We label this as equation (4)

Now we must eliminate the same variable z from another pair of equations by using equation (1) and (3):

$2x + 2y - 2z = -2$ Equation (1) multiplied by 2

$\underline{2x - y + 2z = 9}$ Equation (3) then add both equations

$4x + y \quad\quad = 7$ We label this as equation (5)

We now use both equations (4) and (5) to obtain the value of x:

$5x + y = 5$ Equation (4)

$\underline{-4x - y = -7}$ Equation (5) multiplied by -1

$x \quad\quad = -2$

Substitute x back in to calculate y:

$4x + y = 7$

$4(-2) + y = 7$

$-8 + y = 7$

$y = 15$

Substitute x and y back in to calculate z:

$x + y - z = -1$

$-2 + 15 - z = -1$

$13 - z = -1$

$-z = -14$

$z = 14$

Thus: $x = -2$, $y = 15$, $z = 14$

Question 152: D

This is one of the easier maths questions. Take 3a as a factor to give:

$3a(a^2 - 10a + 25) = 3a(a - 5)(a - 5) = 3a(a - 5)^2$

Question 153: B

Note that 12 is the Lowest Common Multiple of 3 and 4. Thus:

-3 (4x + 3y) = -3 (48)	Multiply each side by -3
4 (3x + 2y) = 4 (34)	Multiply each side by 4
-12x – 9y = -144	
12x + 8y = 136	Add together

$$-y = -8$$
$$y = 8$$

Substitute y back in:

$4x + 3y = 48$

$4x + 3(8) = 48$

$4x + 24 = 48$

$4x = 24$

$x = 6$

Question 154: E

Don't be fooled, this is an easy question, just obey BODMAS and don't skip steps.

$$\frac{-(25-28)^2}{-36+14} = \frac{-(-3)^2}{-22}$$

This gives: $\frac{-(9)}{-22} = \frac{9}{22}$

Question 155: E

Since there are 26 possible letters for each of the 3 letters in the license plate, and there are 10 possible numbers (0-9) for each of the 3 numbers in the same plate, then the number of license plates would be:

$(26) \times (26) \times (26) \times (10) \times (10) \times (10) = 17{,}576{,}000$

Question 156: B

Expand the brackets to give: $4x^2 - 12x + 9 = 0$.

Factorise: $(2x - 3)(2x - 3) = 0$.

Thus, only one solution exists, x = 1.5.

Note that you could also use the fact that the discriminant, $b^2 - 4ac = 0$ to get the answer.

Question 157: C

$$= \left(x^{\frac{1}{2}}\right)^{\frac{1}{2}} (y^{-3})^{\frac{1}{2}}$$

$$= x^{\frac{1}{4}} y^{-\frac{3}{2}} = \frac{x^{\frac{1}{4}}}{y^{\frac{3}{2}}}$$

Question 158: A

Let x, y, and z represent the rent for the 1-bedroom, 2-bedroom, and 3-bedroom flats, respectively. We can write 3 different equations: 1 for the rent, 1 for the repairs, and the last one for the statement that the 3-bedroom unit costs twice as much as the 1-bedroom unit.

(1) $x + y + z = 1240$

(2) $0.1x + 0.2y + 0.3z = 276$

(3) $z = 2x$

Substitute $z = 2x$ in both of the two other equations to eliminate z:

(4) $x + y + 2x = 3x + y = 1240$

(5) $0.1x + 0.2y + 0.3(2x) = 0.7x + 0.2y = 276$

$-2(3x + y) = -2(1240)$	Multiply each side of (4) by -2
$10(0.7x + 0.2y) = 10(276)$	Multiply each side of (5) by 10
(6) $-6x -2y = -2480$	Add these 2 equations
<u>**(7)** $7x + 2y = 2760$</u>	
$x = 280$	
$z = 2(280) = 560$	Because $z = 2x$
$280 + y + 560 = 1240$	Because $x + y + z = 1240$
$y = 400$	

Thus the units rent for £ 280, £ 400, £ 560 per week respectively.

Question 159: C

Following BODMAS:

$$= 5 \left[5(6^2 - 5 \times 3) + 400^{\frac{1}{2}} \right]^{1/3} + 7$$

$$= 5 \left[5(36 - 15) + 20 \right]^{\frac{1}{3}} + 7$$

$$= 5 \left[5(21) + 20 \right]^{\frac{1}{3}} + 7$$

$$= 5 \left(105 + 20 \right)^{\frac{1}{3}} + 7$$

$$= 5 \left(125 \right)^{\frac{1}{3}} + 7$$

$$= 5 (5) + 7$$

$$= 25 + 7 = 32$$

Question 160: B

Consider a triangle formed by joining the centre to two adjacent vertices. Six similar triangles can be made around the centre – thus, the central angle is 60 degrees. Since the two lines forming the triangle are of equal length, we have 6 identical equilateral triangles in the hexagon.

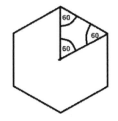

Now split the triangle in half and apply Pythagoras' theorem: $1^2 = 0.5^2 + h^2$

Thus, $h = \sqrt{\frac{3}{4}} = \frac{\sqrt{3}}{2}$

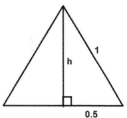

Thus, the area of the triangle is: $\frac{1}{2} bh = \frac{1}{2} \times 1 \times \frac{\sqrt{3}}{2} = \frac{\sqrt{3}}{4}$

Therefore, the area of the hexagon is: $\frac{\sqrt{3}}{4} \times 6 = \frac{3\sqrt{3}}{2}$

Question 161: B

Let x be the width and x+19 be the length.

Thus, the area of a rectangle is x(x + 19) = 780.

Therefore:

$x^2 + 19x - 780 = 0$

$(x - 20)(x + 39) = 0$

$x - 20 = 0$ or $x + 39 = 0$

$x = 20$ or $x = -39$

Since length can never be a negative number, we disregard x = -39 and use x = 20 instead.

Thus, the width is 20 metres and the length is 39 metres.

Question 162: B

The quickest way to solve is by trial and error, substituting the provided options. However, if you're keen to do this algebraically, you can do the following:

Start by setting up the equations: Perimeter = 2L + 2W = 34

Thus: L + W = 17

Using Pythagoras: $L^2 + W^2 = 13^2$

Since L + W = 17, W = 17 - L

Therefore: $L^2 + (17 - L)^2 = 169$

$L^2 + 289 - 34L + L^2 = 169$

$2L^2 - 34L + 120 = 0$

$L^2 - 17L + 60 = 0$

$(L - 5)(L - 12) = 0$

Thus: L = 5 and L = 12

And: W = 12 and W = 5

Question 163: C

Multiply both sides by 8:	$4(3x - 5) + 2(x + 5) = 8(x + 1)$
Remove brackets:	$12x - 20 + 2x + 10 = 8x + 8$
Simplify:	$14x - 10 = 8x + 8$
Add 10:	$14x = 8x + 18$
Subtract 8x:	$6x = 18$
Therefore:	$x = 3$

Question 164: C

Recognise that 1.742 x 3 is 5.226. Now, the original equation simplifies to:

$$= \frac{3 \times 10^6 + 3 \times 10^5}{10^{10}}$$

$$= 3 \times 10^{-4} + 3 \times 10^{-5} = 3.3 \times 10^{-4}$$

Question 165: A

$$Area = \frac{(2 + \sqrt{2})(4 - \sqrt{2})}{2}$$

$$= \frac{8 - 2\sqrt{2} + 4\sqrt{2} - 2}{2}$$

$$= \frac{6 + 2\sqrt{2}}{2}$$

$$= 3 + \sqrt{2}$$

Question 166: C

Square both sides: $\frac{4}{x} + 9 = (y - 2)^2$

$\frac{4}{x} = (y - 2)^2 - 9$

Cross Multiply: $\frac{x}{4} = \frac{1}{(y-2)^2-9}$

$x = \frac{4}{y^2-4y+4-9}$

Factorise: $x = \frac{4}{y^2-4y-5}$

$x = \frac{4}{(y+1)(y-5)}$

Question 167: D
Set up the equation: $5x - 5 = 0.5(6x + 2)$
$10x - 10 = 6x + 2$
$4x = 12$
$x = 3$

Question 168: C

Round numbers appropriately: $\frac{55 + (\frac{9}{4})^2}{\sqrt{900}} = \frac{55 + \frac{81}{16}}{30}$

81 rounds to 80 to give: $\frac{55 + 5}{30} = \frac{60}{30} = 2$

Question 169: D
There are three outcomes from choosing the type of cheese in the crust. For each of the additional toppings to possibly add, there are 2 outcomes: 1 to include and another not to include a certain topping, for each of the 7 toppings
Thus, the number of different kinds of pizza is: 3 x 2 x 2 x 2 x 2 x 2 x 2 x 2
$= 3 \times 2^7$
$= 3 \times 128 = 384$

Question 170: A

Although it is possible to do this algebraically, by far the easiest way is via trial and error. The clue that you shouldn't attempt it algebraically is the fact that rearranging the first equation to make x or y the subject leaves you with a difficult equation to work with (e.g. $x = \sqrt{1 - y^2}$) when you try to substitute in the second.

An exceptionally good student might notice that the equations are symmetric in x and y, i.e. the solution is when x = y. Thus $2x^2 = 1$ and $2x = \sqrt{2}$ which gives $\frac{\sqrt{2}}{2}$ as the answer.

Question 171: C

If two shapes are congruent, then they are the same size and shape. Thus, congruent objects can be rotations and mirror images of each other. The two triangles in E are indeed congruent (SAS). Congruent objects must, by definition, have the same angles.

Question 172: B

Rearrange the equation: $x^2 + x - 6 \geq 0$
Factorise: $(x + 3)(x - 2) \geq 0$
Remember that this is a quadratic inequality so requires a quick sketch to ensure you don't make a silly mistake with which way the sign is.

$y = 0$ when $x = 2$ and $x = -3$.
$y > 0$ when $x > 2$ or $x < -3$.
Thus, $x \leq -3 \ and \ x \geq 2$.

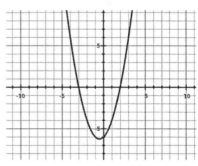

Question 173: B

Using Pythagoras: $a^2 + b^2 = x^2$

Since the triangle is equilateral: $a = b,\ so\ 2a^2 = x^2$

Area $= \frac{1}{2} base\ x\ height = \frac{1}{2}a^2$. From above, $a^2 = \frac{x^2}{2}$

Thus the area $= \frac{1}{2}x\frac{x^2}{2} = \frac{x^2}{4}$

Question 174: A

If X and Y are doubled, the value of Q increases by 4. Halving the value of A reduces this to 2. Finally, tripling the value of B reduces this to ⅔, i.e. the value decreases by ⅓.

Question 175: C

The quickest way to do this is to sketch the curves. This requires you to factorise both equations by completing the square:
$x^2 - 2x + 3 = (x - 1)^2 + 2$
$x^2 - 6x - 10 = (x - 3)^2 - 19$ Thus, the first equation has a turning point at (1, 2) and doesn't cross the x-axis. The second equation has a turning point at (3, -19) and crosses the x-axis twice.

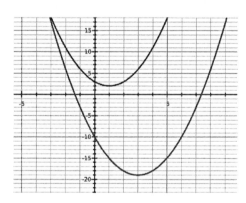

Question 176: C

Segment area $= \frac{60}{360}\pi r^2 = \frac{1}{6}\pi r^2$

$\frac{x}{\sin 30°} = \frac{2r}{\sin 60°}$

$x = \frac{2r}{\sqrt{3}}$

Total triangle area $= 2 \times \frac{1}{2} \times \frac{2r}{\sqrt{3}} \times 2r = \frac{4r^2}{\sqrt{3}}$

Proportion covered: $\frac{1}{6}\pi r^2 / \frac{4r^2}{\sqrt{3}} = \frac{\sqrt{3}\pi}{24} \approx 23\%$

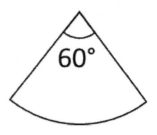

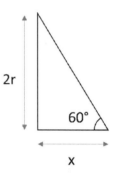

Question 177: B

$(2r)^2 = r^2 + x^2$

$3r^2 = x^2$

$x = \sqrt{3}r$

$Total\ height = 2r + x = (2 + \sqrt{3})r$

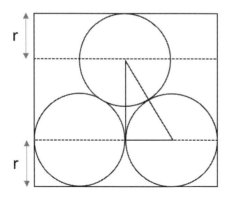

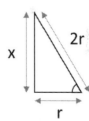

Question 178: A

$V = \frac{1}{3}h \times$ base area

Therefore base area must be equal if h and V are the same

Internal angle $= 180° -$ external ; external $= 360°/6 = 60°$ giving internal angle $120°$

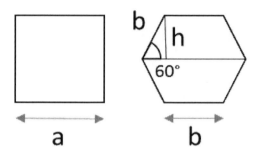

Hexagon is two trapezia of height h where: $\dfrac{b}{\sin 90°} = \dfrac{h}{\sin 60°}$

$h = \dfrac{\sqrt{3}}{2}b$

Trapezium area $= \dfrac{(2b+b)}{2}\dfrac{\sqrt{3}}{2}b = \dfrac{3\sqrt{3}}{4}b^2$

Total hexagon area $= \dfrac{3\sqrt{3}}{2}b^2$

So from equal volumes: $a^2 = \dfrac{3\sqrt{3}}{2}b^2$

Ratio: $\sqrt{\dfrac{3\sqrt{3}}{2}}$

Question 179: C

A cube has 6 sides so the Area of 9 cm cube $= 6 \times 9^2$

9 cm cube splits into 3 cm cubes.

Area of 3 cm cubes $= 3^3 \times 6 \times 9^2$

$\dfrac{6\times3^2\times3^3}{6\times3^2\times3^2} = 3$

Question 180: C

$x^2 = (4r)^2 + r^2$

$x = \sqrt{17}r$

$\dfrac{\sqrt{17}r}{\sin 90°} = \dfrac{r}{\sin \theta}$

$\theta = \sin^{-1}\left(\dfrac{1}{\sqrt{17}}\right)$

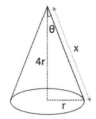

Question 181: C

0 to 200 is 180 degrees so: $\dfrac{\theta}{180} = \dfrac{70}{200}$

$\theta = \dfrac{7 \times 180}{20} = 63°$

Question 182: A

Since the rhombi are similar, the ratio of angles = 1

Length scales with square root of area so length B = $\sqrt{10}$ length A

$\dfrac{\text{angle } A\big/\text{angle } B}{\text{length } A\big/\text{length } B} = \dfrac{1}{\sqrt{10}\big/1} = \dfrac{1}{\sqrt{10}}$

Question 183: E

$y = \ln (2x^2)$

$e^y = 2x^2$

$x = \sqrt{\dfrac{e^y}{2}}$

As the input is -x, the inverse function must be $f(x) = -\sqrt{\dfrac{e^y}{2}}$

Question 184: C

$log_8(x)$ and $log_{10}(x) < 0$; $x^2 < 1$; $\sin(x) \leq 1$ and $1 < e^x < 2.72$

So e^x is largest over this range

Question 185: C

$x \propto \sqrt{z}^{-3}$

$\sqrt{2}^{-3} = 2\sqrt{2}$

Question 186: A

The area of the larger circle, radius x, must be 4x the smaller one so:

$4\pi r^2 = \pi x^2$

$4r^2 = x^2$

$x = 2r$

The gap is $x - r = 2r - r = r$

Question 187: B

$0 \geq x^2 + 3x - 4$

$0 \geq (x - 1)(x + 4)$

$0 \geq x - 1$ or $0 \geq x + 4$

So $x \leq 1$ or $x \leq -4$

Question 188: C

$\frac{4}{3}\pi r^3 = \pi r^2$

$\frac{4}{3}r = 1$

$r = \frac{3}{4}$

Question 189: B

When $x^2 = \frac{1}{x}$; $x = 1$

When $x > 1, x^2 > 1, \frac{1}{x} < 1$

When $x < 1, x^2 < 1, \frac{1}{x} > 1$

Range for $\frac{1}{x}$ is $x > 0$

Non-inclusive so: $0 < x < 1$

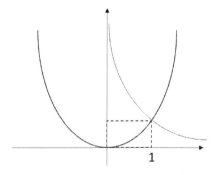

Question 190: D

Subtract line 2 from 3: $\begin{pmatrix} -1 & 2 & -1 \\ 2 & 1 & 3 \\ 0 & -2 & 1 \end{pmatrix}\begin{pmatrix} x \\ y \\ z \end{pmatrix} = \begin{pmatrix} 1 \\ 7 \\ 2 \end{pmatrix}$

Add 2x line 1 to line 2: $\begin{pmatrix} -1 & 2 & -1 \\ 0 & 5 & 1 \\ 0 & -2 & 1 \end{pmatrix}\begin{pmatrix} x \\ y \\ z \end{pmatrix} = \begin{pmatrix} 1 \\ 9 \\ 2 \end{pmatrix}$

Add 2xline 2 to 5x line 3: $\begin{pmatrix} -1 & 2 & -1 \\ 0 & 5 & 1 \\ 0 & 0 & 7 \end{pmatrix}\begin{pmatrix} x \\ y \\ z \end{pmatrix} = \begin{pmatrix} 1 \\ 9 \\ 28 \end{pmatrix}$

[Can be done via substitution from hereon]: $\begin{pmatrix} -1 & 2 & -1 \\ 0 & 5 & 1 \\ 0 & 0 & 1 \end{pmatrix}\begin{pmatrix} x \\ y \\ z \end{pmatrix} = \begin{pmatrix} 1 \\ 9 \\ 4 \end{pmatrix}$

Subtract line 3 from line 2 and add line 3 to line 1:

$$\begin{pmatrix} -1 & 2 & 0 \\ 0 & 5 & 0 \\ 0 & 0 & 1 \end{pmatrix}\begin{pmatrix} x \\ y \\ z \end{pmatrix} = \begin{pmatrix} 5 \\ 5 \\ 4 \end{pmatrix}$$

$$\begin{pmatrix} -1 & 2 & 0 \\ 0 & 1 & 0 \\ 0 & 0 & 1 \end{pmatrix}\begin{pmatrix} x \\ y \\ z \end{pmatrix} = \begin{pmatrix} 5 \\ 1 \\ 4 \end{pmatrix}$$

Subtract 2 x line 2 from line 1:

$$\begin{pmatrix} -1 & 0 & 0 \\ 0 & 1 & 0 \\ 0 & 0 & 1 \end{pmatrix}\begin{pmatrix} x \\ y \\ z \end{pmatrix} = \begin{pmatrix} 3 \\ 1 \\ 4 \end{pmatrix}$$

$$\begin{pmatrix} 1 & 0 & 0 \\ 0 & 1 & 0 \\ 0 & 0 & 1 \end{pmatrix}\begin{pmatrix} x \\ y \\ z \end{pmatrix} = \begin{pmatrix} -3 \\ 1 \\ 4 \end{pmatrix}$$

Question 191: C

For two vectors to be perpendicular their scalar product must be equal to 0.

Hence, $\begin{pmatrix} -1 \\ 6 \end{pmatrix} \cdot \begin{pmatrix} 2 \\ k \end{pmatrix} = 0$

$\therefore \; -2 + 6k = 0$

$k = \frac{1}{3}$

Question 192: C

The point, q, in the plane meets the perpendicular line from the plane to the point p.

$q = -3i + j + \lambda_1 (i + 2j)$

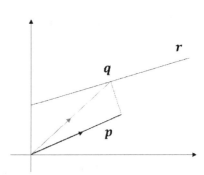

$\overrightarrow{PQ} = -3i + j + \lambda_1 (i + 2j) + 4i + 5j$

$= \begin{pmatrix} -7 + \lambda_1 \\ -4 + 2\lambda_1 \end{pmatrix}$

PQ is perpendicular to the plane r

therefore the dot product of $\overrightarrow{PQ}$ and a vector within the plane must be 0.

$\begin{pmatrix} -7 + \lambda_1 \\ -4 + 2\lambda_1 \end{pmatrix} \cdot \begin{pmatrix} 1 \\ 2 \end{pmatrix} = 0$

$\therefore \; -7 + \lambda_1 - 8 + 4 + \lambda_1 = 0$

$\lambda_1 = 3$

$\overrightarrow{PQ} = \begin{pmatrix} -4 \\ 2 \end{pmatrix}$

The perpendicular distance from the plane to point p is therefore the modulus of the vector joining the two $\overrightarrow{PQ}$:

$|\overrightarrow{PQ}| = \sqrt{(-4)^2 + 2^2} = \sqrt{20} = 2\sqrt{5}$

Question 193: E

$-1 + 3\mu = -7 \; ; \; \mu = -2$

$2 + 4\lambda + 2\mu = 2 \; \therefore \; \lambda = 1$

$3 + \lambda + \mu = k \; \therefore \; k = 2$

Question 194: E

$\sin\left(\frac{\pi}{2} - 2\theta\right) = \cos(2\theta)$

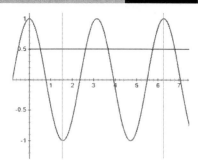

Root solution to $\cos(\theta) = 0.5$

$\theta = \frac{\pi}{3}$

Solution to $\cos(2\theta) = 0.5$

$\theta = \frac{\pi}{6}$

Largest solution within range is: $2\pi - \frac{\pi}{6} = \frac{(12-1)\pi}{6} = \frac{11\pi}{6}$

Question 195: A

$\cos^4(x) - \sin^4(x) \equiv \{\cos^2(x) - \sin^2(x)\}\{\cos^2(x) + \sin^2(x)\}$

From difference of two squares, then using Pythagorean identity $\cos^2(x) + \sin^2(x) = 1$

$\cos^4(x) - \sin^4(x) \equiv \cos^2(x) - \sin^2(x)$

But double angle formula says: $\cos(A + B) = \cos(A)\cos(B) - \sin(A)\sin(B)$

$\therefore if \; A = B, \cos(2A) = \cos(A)\cos(A) - \sin(A)\sin(A)$

$= \cos^2(A) - \sin^2(A)$

So, $\cos^4(x) - \sin^4(x) \equiv \cos(2x)$

Question 196: C

Factorise: $(x + 1)(x + 2)(2x - 1)(x^2 + 2) = 0$

Three real roots at $x = -1, x = -2, x = 0.5$ and two imaginary roots at 2i and -2i

Question 197: C
An arithmetic sequence has constant difference d so the sum increases by d
more each time:

$$u_n = u_1 + (n-1)d$$
$$\sum_1^n u_n = \frac{n}{2}\{2u_1 + (n-1)d\}$$
$$\sum_1^8 u_n = \frac{8}{2}\{4 + (8-1)3\} = 100$$

Question 198: E

$$\binom{n}{k} 2^{n-k}(-x)^k = \binom{5}{2} 2^{5-2}(-x)^2$$
$$= 10 \times 2^3 x^2 = 80x^2$$

Question 199: A
Having already thrown a 6 is irrelevant. A fair die has equal probability
$$P = \frac{1}{6} \text{ for every throw.}$$
For three throws: $P(6 \cap 6 \cap 6) = \left(\frac{1}{6}\right)^3 = \frac{1}{216}$

Question 200: D

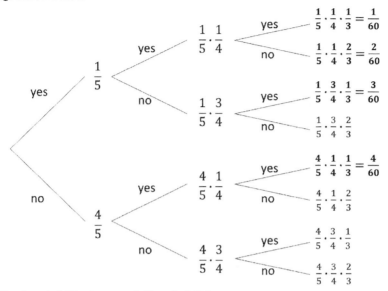

Total probability is sum of all probabilities:

$= P(Y \cap Y \cap Y) + P(Y \cap Y \cap N) + P(Y \cap N \cap Y) + P(N \cap Y \cap Y)$

$= \frac{1}{60} + \frac{2}{60} + \frac{3}{60} + \frac{4}{60} = \frac{10}{60} = \frac{1}{6}$

Question 201: C

$P[(A \cup B)'] = 1 - P[(A \cup B)]$

$= 1 - \{P(A) + P(B) - P(A \cap B)\}$

$= 1 - \frac{2+6-1}{8} = \frac{3}{8}$

Question 202: E

Using the product rule: $\frac{dy}{dx} = x \cdot 4(x + 3)^3 + 1 \cdot (x + 3)^4$

$= 4x(x + 3)^3 + (x + 3)(x + 3)^3$

$= (5x + 3)(x + 3)^3$

Question 203: C

$\int_1^2 \frac{2}{x^2}\,dx = \int_1^2 2x^{-2}\,dx =$

$\left[\frac{2x^{-1}}{-1}\right]_1^2 = \left[\frac{-2}{x}\right]_1^2$

$= \frac{-2}{2} - \frac{-2}{1} = 1$

Question 204: D

Express $\frac{5i}{1+2i}$ in the form $a + bi$

$\frac{5i}{1+2i} \cdot \frac{1-2i}{1-2i}$

$= \frac{5i+10}{1+4} - \frac{5i+10}{5}$

$= i + 2$

Question 205: B

$7\log_a(2) - 3\log_a(12) + 5\log_a(3)$

$7\log_a(2) = \log_a(2^7) = \log_a(128)$

$3\log_a(12) = \log_a(1728)$

$5\log_a(3) = \log_a(243)$

This gives: $\log_a(128) - \log_a(1728) + \log_a(243)$

$= \log_a\left(\frac{128 \times 243}{1728}\right) = \log_a(18)$

Question 206: E

Functions of the form quadratic over quadratic have a horizontal asymptote. Divide each term by the highest order in the polynomial i.e. x^2:

$$\frac{2x^2 - x + 3}{x^2 + x - 2} = \frac{2 - \frac{1}{x} + \frac{3}{x^2}}{1 + \frac{1}{x} - \frac{2}{x^2}}$$

$$\lim_{x \to \infty}\left(\frac{2 - \frac{1}{x} + \frac{3}{x^2}}{1 + \frac{1}{x} - \frac{2}{x^2}}\right) = \frac{2}{1} \ i.e. \ y \to 2$$

So the asymptote is $y = 2$

Question 207: A

$1 - 3e^{-x} = e^x - 3$

$4 = e^x + 3e^{-x} = \frac{(e^x)^2}{e^x} + \frac{3}{e^x} = \frac{(e^x)^2 + 3}{e^x}$

This is a quadratic equation in (e^x): $(e^x)^2 - 4(e^x) + 3 = 0$

$(e^x - 3)(e^x - 1) = 0$

So $e^x = 3, x = \ln(3)$ or $e^x = 1, x = 0$

Question 208: C

Rearrange into the format: $(x + a)^2 + (y + b)^2 = r^2$

$(x - 3)^2 + (y + 4)^2 - 25 = 12$

$(x - 3)^2 + (y + 4)^2 = 37$

$\therefore r = \sqrt{37}$

Question 209: D

$\sin(-x) = -\sin(x)$

$\int_0^a 2\sin(-x)\,dx = -2\int_0^a \sin(x)\,dx = -2[\cos(x)]_0^a = \cos(a) - 1$

Solve $\cos(a) - 1 = 0 \therefore a = 2k\pi$

Or simply the integral of any whole period of $\sin(x) = 0$ i.e. $a = 2k\pi$

Question 210: E

$\frac{2x+3}{(x-2)(x-3)^2} = \frac{A}{(x-2)} + \frac{B}{(x-3)} + \frac{C}{(x-3)^2}$

$2x + 3 = A(x - 3)^2 + B(x - 2)(x - 3) + C(x - 2)$

When $x = 3, (x - 3) = 0$, $C = 9$

When $x = 2, (x - 2) = 0$, $A = 7$

$2x + 3 = 7(x - 3)^2 + B(x - 2)(x - 3) + 9(x - 2)$

For completeness: Equating coefficients of x^2 on either side: $0 = 7 + B$ which gives: $B = -7$

Section 2 Worked Solutions

Q	A	Q	A	Q	A	Q	A	Q	A
1.1	C	3.1	B	5.1	C	7.1	D	9.1	A
1.2	D	3.2	E	5.2	B	7.2	B	9.2	E
1.3	C	3.3	B	5.3	A	7.3	C	9.3	E
1.4	C	3.4	D	5.4	C	7.4	B	9.4	D
2.1	A	4.1	E	6.1	E	8.1	E	10.1	B
2.2	E	4.2	B	6.2	A	8.2	A	10.2	E
2.3	D	4.3	C	6.3	B	8.3	D	10.3	B
2.4	A	4.4	E	6.4	A	8.4	B	10.4	D

Question 1.1: C
The distance the ball travels is maximised when the angle to the horizontal at which the golfer hits the ball is 45°.

Question 1.2: D
The velocity at which the golfer hits the ball is $\frac{2\pi L}{T} = 62.5$m/s.

Question 1.3: C
Vertical velocity is $v sin(45)$, acceleration is downwards $g = -10$
The time t the ball spends in the air is twice the time to reach peak height when v= 0. $\Delta v = at$; $t = 2v\frac{sin(45°)}{g} = 6\sqrt{2}$

Question 1.4: C
Time spent for vertical motion is the same as that for horizontal. Assuming air resistance is negligible. The distance D the ball travels in that time is then $D = v_h t = vcos(45°)t = 360\ m$.

Question 2.1: A

The mass of the Moon is $M_{Moon} = \rho_{Moon} * V_{Moon} = \rho_{Moon} * 4r_{Moon}^3 \pi/3$

As density and radius are different, substitute in for $(3/4)$ ρ and $(1/4)$r to make it in terms of the earth's data: $\frac{3}{4}\rho_{earth} \times 4 \times \frac{3}{4}r_{earth^3} \times \frac{\pi}{3}$

Question 2.2: E

The gravitational acceleration is $= \frac{GM}{R^2}$. Then $g_{Earth} = G\rho(\frac{4}{3})\pi r$

Question 2.3: D

Take the ratio of the two and simplify gives $g_{moon} = (\frac{3}{16})g_{earth}$

Question 2.4: A

$F = mg = mv^2/r$ for a satellite. So v is proportional to the square root of g therefore the speed will decrease with decreased g by a factor of $\sqrt{\frac{3}{16}}$.

Question 3.1: B

$\frac{1}{Rtotal} = \frac{1}{R} + \frac{1}{R}$ $therefore$ $Rtotal = \frac{R}{2}$

Question 3.2: E

Evaluate each group in parallel as one component and then add in series to first:

$$R_{total} = R + \cfrac{1}{\cfrac{1}{R+\frac{1}{\frac{1}{R}+\frac{1}{R}}} + \cfrac{1}{R+\frac{1}{\frac{1}{R}+\frac{1}{R}}}}$$

$$= R + \cfrac{1}{\frac{2}{R+R/2}} = R + \cfrac{1}{\frac{2}{3R/2}} = R + \frac{3R}{4} = 7R/4$$

Question 3.3: B

$V = IR_{total;}$ Use total resistance from previous question

Question 3.4: D

$P = VI$ using total current and voltage from previous

Question 4.1: E
Snell's law: $n_1/\sin\theta_1 = n_2/\sin\theta_2$.

Question 4.2: B
Angle of incidence is measured from the ray to the normal to the interface. When the angle of incidence reaches a certain critical value, the refracted ray lies along the boundary, having an angle of refraction of 90-degrees. This angle of incidence is known as the critical angle; it is the largest angle of incidence for which refraction can still occur. In this diagram the angle is B.

Question 4.3: C
$\sin(\theta_{critical}) = n_g\sin(90°)/n_c$; $\theta_{critical} = 68.8°$

Question 4.4: E
There is no critical angle as going from larger to smaller n as light is bent towards the normal so total internal reflection is not possible

Question 5.1: C
Gravitational potential energy = mgh
$= (700 + 800) \; x \; 10 \; x \; 7 \; = 105,000 \, J$

Question 5.2: B
Power = Energy / Time = 3500 W
Assuming 100% efficiency, energy put in is gravitational potential from previous

Question 5.3: A
Average velocity = Distance / Time $=0.23 \text{ ms}^{-1}$
$Kinetic \; energy \; = \frac{mv^2}{2} = \; 40.8 \, J$

Question 5.4: C
The lift accelerates with the acceleration a for t=10 s, then it uniformly moves for t=10 s with the speed $v=at$ and then it decelerates with the same acceleration for t=10s.

$$h = \frac{at^2}{2} + vt + \frac{at^2}{2} = 2at^2 = 2vt$$
$$v = \frac{H}{2t} = 0.35\ ms^{-1}$$

Question 6.1: E
$m_2a_2 = m_2g\ sin\alpha - \mu_2m_2g\ cos\alpha => a_2 = g\ (sin\alpha - \mu_2cos\alpha)$

Question 6.2: A
$m_1a_1 = m_1g\ sin\alpha - \mu_1m_1g\ cos\alpha => a_1 = g\ (sin\alpha - \mu_1cos\alpha)$

Question 6.3: B
$a_1' = a_1 - a_2 = g\ cos\alpha\ (\mu_1 - \mu_2)$

Question 6.4: A
When forces balance $m_2g\ sin\alpha = \mu_2m_2g\ cos\alpha$ so $\mu_2 = \frac{sin\alpha}{cos\alpha} = tan\alpha$

Question 7.1: D
Magnification= image height/object height = 2
i/o=h'/h=2 so object is 8 cm from lens

Question 7.2: B
We use $\frac{1}{a} + \frac{1}{b} = \frac{1}{f}$ where a is the distance from the (real or virtual) object to the lens, b is the distance between the lens, and f is the focal length of the lens.

For the second lens we have $\frac{1}{a_2} + \frac{1}{b_2} = \frac{1}{f_2}$ where $b_2 = 5cm => a_2 = -10$ cm

Question 7.3: C
This means that the first lens forms an image of the object behind the second lens so that $b_1 = d - b_2 = 40$ cm

For the first lens we have $\frac{1}{a_1} + \frac{1}{b_1} = \frac{1}{f_1} => a_2 = 40$ cm

Question 7.4: B
Both are the opposite side of the lens to the object therefore real and inverted

Question 8.1: E
The charge inside a sphere of radius $r<R$ is:

$$q(r < R) = \int_o^r 4\pi r^2 \rho dr = \int_o^r 4\pi r^3 a dr = a\pi r^4$$

Question 8.2: A
The electric potential inside the sphere is then $E\ (r<R) = \dfrac{a\pi r^4}{4\pi\varepsilon r^2} = \dfrac{ar^2}{4\varepsilon}$

Question 8.3: D
For total charge in the sphere, set r=R in answer from 8.1 so $Q = a\pi R^4$

Question 8.4: B
Therefore, the electric field outside the sphere is:
$$E\ (r>R) = \frac{a\pi R^4}{4\pi\varepsilon r^2} = \frac{aR^4}{4\varepsilon r^2}$$

Question 9.1: A
The total spring constant is simply the sum as they are in series $k=k_1+k_2$

Question 9.2: E
Each of the springs experiences the same force as they are in series
$F=k_1 l_1 = k_2 l_2$
$\Rightarrow l_1 = k_2 l_2 / k_1$

where l_1 and l_2 are the extensions of the spring 1 and 2 respectively

Question 9.3: E
We can see that $l_1 < l_2$ since $k_2 < k_1$. This means that when $l_2 = l$ (just before the spring 2 breaks) the extension of spring 1 is $l_1 = k_2 l / k_1$, e.g. the spring 2 puts the limit on the extension of the spring 1 that is smaller than l.

Question 9.4: D
We can obtain the maximum speed of oscillations from the conservation of energy: $mv_{max}/2 = (k_1 l_1^2 + k_2 l_2^2)/2 \Rightarrow v_{max} = \dfrac{(k_1+k_2)k_2 l^2}{k_1 m}$

Question 10.1: B
Where r is the distance from the charge.
At the centre, $r = \sqrt{\dfrac{3a}{4}}$ for all three charges.

Question 10.2: E
Each charge produces an electric field of magnitude:

$$|E| = \frac{q}{4\pi\epsilon_0 r^2}$$

Only the two positive charges have non-zero horizontal components at the centre, both with a magnitude of $|E|cos30°$, but of opposite signs so they cancel each other out.

Question 10.3: B
In the vertical direction, the electric field at the centre of the triangle is:

$$|E| = \frac{q}{4\pi\epsilon_0 (\sqrt{3a/4})^2} [2\sin 30 - (-1)] = \frac{8q}{3\pi\epsilon_0 a^2}$$

Question 10.4: D
If all the charges had the same sign, the electric field at the centre would be zero because the two terms in the brackets in the expression for the electric field in the vertical direction would cancel each other out.

Final Advice

Arrive well rested, well fed and well hydrated

The ENGAA is an intensive test, so make sure you're ready for it. Unlike the ENGAA, you'll have to sit this at a fixed time (normally at 9AM). Thus, ensure you get a good night's sleep before the exam (there is little point cramming) and don't miss breakfast. If you're taking water into the exam then make sure you've been to the toilet before so you don't have to leave during the exam. Make sure you're well rested and fed in order to be at your best!

Move on

If you're struggling, move on. In the time it takes to answer on hard question, you could gain three times the marks by answering the easier ones. Be smart to score points- especially in section 2 where some questions are far easier than others and different questions are worth different marks.

Afterword

Remember that the route to a high score is your approach and practice. Don't fall into the trap that *"you can't prepare for the ENGAA"*– this could not be further from the truth. With knowledge of the test, some useful time-saving techniques and plenty of practice you can dramatically boost your score.

Work hard, never give up and do yourself justice.

Good luck!

Acknowledgements

I would like to express my sincerest thanks to the many people who helped make this book possible, especially the Oxbridge Tutors who shared their expertise in compiling the huge number of questions and answers.

Rohan

About UniAdmissions

UniAdmissions is an educational consultancy that specialises in supporting **applications to Medical School and to Oxbridge**.

Every year, we work with hundreds of applicants and schools across the UK. From free resources to our *Ultimate Guide Books* and from intensive courses to bespoke individual tuition – with a team of **300 Expert Tutors** and a proven track record, it's easy to see why UniAdmissions is the **UK's number one admissions company**.

To find out more about our support like **ENGAA tuition** check out www.uniadmissions.co.uk/ENGAA

Your Free Book

Thanks for purchasing this Ultimate Guide Book. Readers like you have the power to make or break a book – hopefully you found this one useful and informative. *UniAdmissions* would love to hear about your experiences with this book.

As thanks for your time we'll send you another ebook from our Ultimate Guide series absolutely <u>FREE</u>!

How to Redeem Your Free Ebook

1) Find the book you have either on your Amazon purchase history or your email receipt to help find the book on Amazon.

2) On the product page at the Customer Reviews area, click 'Write a customer review'. Write your review and post it! Copy the review page or take a screen shot of the review you have left.

3) Head over to www.uniadmissions.co.uk/free-book and select your chosen free ebook! You can choose from:

➢ The Ultimate UKCAT Guide
➢ The Ultimate BMAT Guide
➢ The Ultimate TSA Guide
➢ The Ultimate LNAT Guide
➢ The Ultimate NSAA Guide
➢ The Ultimate ECAA Guide
➢ The Ultimate ENGAA Guide
➢ The Ultimate PBSAA Guide
➢ The Ultimate FPAS SJT Guide
➢ The Ultimate Oxbridge Interview Guide

➢ The Ultimate Medical School Interview Guide
➢ The Ultimate UCAS Personal Statement Guide
➢ The Ultimate Medical Personal Statement Guide
➢ The Ultimate Medical School Application Guide
➢ BMAT Past Paper Solutions
➢ TSA Past Paper Worked Solutions

Your ebook will then be emailed to you – it's as simple as that!
Alternatively, you can buy all the above titles at **www.uniadmisions.co.uk/our-books**

C000172150

Walks in
Shakespeare
Country

Explore by Paw Warwickshire

Explore by Paw

If your dog loves a good walk, why not join the Explore by Paw Warwickshire dog walking group?
- Walks are led by experienced walk leaders
- Walks start/finish at dog-friendly pubs
- Weekend and weekday walks
- Member discounts on outdoor gear
- Explore the Warwickshire countryside with new friends

New members with sociable dogs always welcome!

Find us at: www.meetup.com/explore-by-paw-warwickshire

Walks in Shakespeare Country

Twenty-four walks from
dog-friendly pubs near
Stratford-upon-Avon

Lezli Rees

First published in September 2015 by Laughing Dog Media
The Studio, 205 High Street, Henley-in-Arden, Warwickshire

ISBN 978-0-9927197-3-9

Text, maps and photographs © Lezli Rees 2015

British Library Cataloguing in-publication data.

A catalogue is available for this book from the British Library.

Whilst every effort has been made to ensure the information in this book is correct, the author or the publisher can accept no responsibility for errors, loss or injury however caused.

Maps based on Open Street map data.

The countryside is constantly changing and if you wish to alert the publishers to changes to any of these routes we'd be grateful. Please e-mail: warks@drivingwithdogs.co.uk

Contents

Map of Shakespeare Country

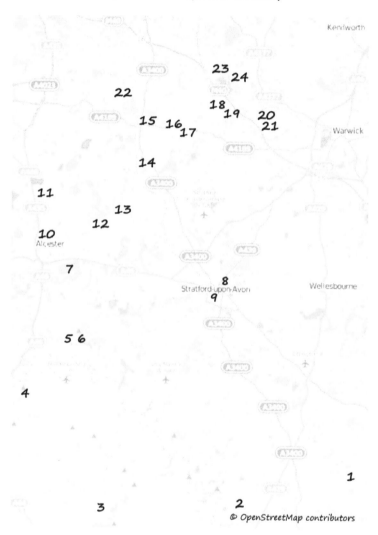

Kenilworth

23
24
22
18
19
15 16 20
17 21
Warwick

14

11

13
12
10
Alcester

7

8
Stratford-upon-Avon   Wellesbourne
9

5 6

4

1

3   2
© OpenStreetMap contributors

Introduction

Every year millions of visitors flock to Stratford-upon-Avon, to the theatre and the historic buildings connected with William Shakespeare. But it's only by walking beside the River Avon and across fields divided by fragrant hedgerows and edged with wild flowers that the subtle charm of the landscapes that inspired Shakespeare slowly draws you in to the poet's world.

Warwickshire could be described as a private and personal region. You won't find the dramatic peaks and valleys of the national parks, on display for all to see. Instead the story here unravels slowly, gently and offers a series of small treasures rather than monumental vistas.

For walkers, this means that you won't find vertiginous hills to climb or steep sided valleys to slither down. The terrain is kind to your feet, and howling moorland winds have no place. Walkers of all abilities and experience are able to complete these walks with ease.

Shakespeare Country is a concept, rather than a clearly defined geographic area. I've interpreted it to mean places within easy reach of Stratford-upon-Avon, and where it is more likely than not that Shakespeare and his family had a definite connection to the locality. Although this isn't intended to be a scholarly guide to the bard's footsteps.

The walks in this book have been selected for two main reasons. First, because they are interesting for walkers, either for scenes of natural beauty or historical interest – not only Shakespeare but also for tangible connections to the Gunpowder Plot, mysterious pre-historic sites and a ghostly Civil War experience. And second, because these walks are easily manageable by walkers who prefer to avoid stiles, livestock and road walking, with or without a dog.

Walk lengths vary from 3 miles to a couple of longer 6 mile walks. Most of the walks are around 5 miles, and these will be easily managed by walkers of average fitness within two hours or so. With the exception of two there-and-back linear walks, the routes are either circular or 'lollipop' shaped in order to avoid particularly awkward stiles, or fields with a high probability of unwelcoming livestock.

To make it easy to follow the walk routes, each instruction is accompanied by a photograph showing which way to go. The photos are also handy for getting the idea of the walk before you set off. The idea of illustrating the walks came from the Explore by Paw dog walking group, and you'll see members of the group walking the routes with their dogs in the photos.

Dog walkers need to know about roads and sheep so that their dogs can be put on-lead for safety; and the whereabouts of dog waste bins is important too. If you don't have a dog, I hope these additions aren't annoying.

Each walk has a small map showing the general route and shape of the walk. This is included merely to show the context and shape of the walk, and not to replace an Ordnance Survey map. These maps are modified versions of open source maps created by the OpenStreetMap project, a community of mappers who contribute and maintain data about roads, trails, cafés, railway stations, and much more, all over the world. To find out more about the project, visit: www.openstreetmap.org.

I'd like to thank all the members of Explore by Paw Warwickshire, who have walked these routes with me and made the process of finding the perfect walk so much more enjoyable. In particular, thanks are due to Paula and Rowan, Tanya and Freddy, Jo and Bo, Carla and Merlin, Tracey and Mitsi, Kate and

Rosie, Jacqui and Lola, Sue and Bruno and especially my husband David with our rescue collie, Jem.

Thanks are also due to the kind and generous landlords of the pubs on the walks. Even when confronted with a group of wet and bedraggled walkers, with muddy dogs to match, their genuine welcome – along with big log fires and excellent food – has been greatly appreciated. Maybe now is the time to apologise for those many wet paw-prints on your freshly scrubbed flagstones.

Whether you're visiting Shakespeare country for the first time, or you're a local resident wishing to explore more of our lovely countryside, I hope you enjoy these walks and country inns and the very special county that is Warwickshire.

Lezli Rees
September 2015

Walk 1
Ratley and Edge Hill

Refreshments: The Rose and Crown, Ratley, Warwickshire, OX15 6DS. Tel: 01295 678148
Opening hours and menus: www.roseandcrown-ratley.co.uk

Parts of the Rose and Crown date back to 1098, and it's been an inn for well over 300 years. Today the Rose and Crown welcomes walkers and dogs, and serves very good food and local beers. In winter you'll find a roaring wood-burner to toast your toes, and the outside beer garden is a lovely sun-trap in summer.

Walk map

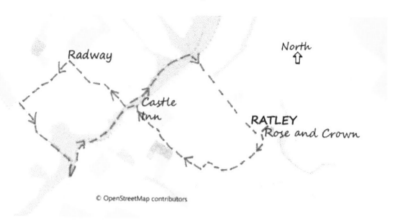

Radway

North ⇧

Castle Inn

RATLEY
Rose and Crown

© OpenStreetMap contributors

Walk info

An atmospheric walk from Ratley, through woodland on Edge Hill with views over to the site of the first pitched battle of the 17th century civil war.

Length: 3 miles (5km)
Stiles: 3
Livestock: sheep likely in one small field, cows possible in another field
Suggested OS map: Explorer 206 Edge Hill and Fenny Compton
Parking: Village hall car park, or on-street near the Rose and Crown OX15 6DS
Nearest vet: Hawthorne Lodge Vet Practice, 1 West Bar Street, Banbury, OX16 9SD
Tel: 01295 259446 (24hr)
Waste bins: in Ratley village

Start point: The Rose and Crown, Ratley OS map: SP384473

Walk 1 Route

Walk from the Rose and Crown to pass the church of St Peter ad Vinculum on your left. Just after a 'Church Street' sign turn left onto a farm track.

Go over a stone stile to the right of a farm gate just after Mount Farm Cottage.

Notice the base of a long-ruined medieval motte and bailey castle on the right, opposite Mount Farm. The castle was built in the mid-12th century, but quickly fell into disuse.

Follow the well-trodden footpath up a small mound and downhill, to cross the second stile (or through the adjacent gate) into a further field where the path leads uphill again.

At the end of this field cross a stile and turn right onto a farm track. This will bring you to a country lane where you turn right. After 30m turn left onto a leafy footpath. This is a narrow path, fenced on both sides, and after passing around buildings will bring you to a road opposite the Castle Inn.

Cross the road with care and take the signed footpath opposite, to the right of the Castle Inn. This is Castle Wood. When the path forks, by a number of footpath arrows, take the left fork and head downhill through the trees.

3

The first big battle of the 1642 civil war took place on fields beyond Radway, below the Castle Inn, and its 18th century octagonal tower-folly is built on the spot where King Charles 1 is said to have watched the battle taking place on the plain below. The result of the battle was inconclusive, but some 1,500 soldiers lost their lives. Sightings of ghosts were reported soon after the battle, and Edge Hill is still considered one of the 'most haunted' parts of Warwickshire.

When you reach the path T-junction at the edge of the trees, go straight on and through the wooden gate into a field.

Continue downhill across this field and go through the gate ahead by a pond.

Keep the fence to your left, and leave the field to join a track leading to the edge of Radway village.

Keep straight on past the charming cottages to reach a wooden signpost pointing left towards King John's Lane.

Turn left as signed, at first along a narrow path edged with headstones and then cross two fields with a kissing gate and plank bridge between them. In the second field, keep the hedge to your right and be prepared for sheep. Go through a kissing gate and follow the narrow path beside a private garden.

Turn left to walk up King John's Lane. This is an ancient trackway, and the name suggests it may have been used by King John on a 13th century royal tour.

Follow the steep track back into Castle Wood.

At the top of the hill turn hairpin left on the clear woodland path. If you reach a waymarker post you've missed the left turn and gone a few metres too far.

Stay on the woodland path as it wriggles through the trees. Pass the wooden gate of your outward route to the left. You may spot an obelisk in a field on the left, and after this stay on the lower woodland path as far as the next wooden gate.

A few metres after this gate, turn right to ascend Edge Hill on a slope and then a set of steps marked on the OS map as 'Jacobs Ladder'. Cross the road at the top with care, and then walk down the lane ahead to return to Ratley.

Walk 2
Ilmington to Newbold-on-Stour

Refreshments at the half-way point: The White Hart, Stratford Road, Newbold-on-Stour, CV37 8TS. Tel: 01789 450205 Opening hours and menus: www.whitehartnewbold.co.uk

The White Hart is a traditional coaching inn, with enormous fireplaces, wooden beams and flagstones. Just the place to head to on a crisp winter's day for a hearty meal and a good warm up. While you're there, don't miss the chance to try your luck at 'Ringing the Bull' – a pub game that looks deceptively easy, but has been tantalising players for centuries.

Walk map

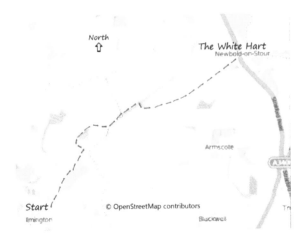

Walk info

A lovely linear walk on well-defined paths and tracks. The advantage of this route is that there are no hills, and yet you get some great views of the start of the Cotswold Hills. Ilmington is a particularly charming village, the highest in Warwickshire, and a delight to explore at the end of your walk.

Allow 50-60 minutes to reach the White Hart at Newbold, and check your timings to avoid arriving before the 12 noon opening time.

Length: 6 miles (9.5km)
Stiles: 0
Livestock: sheep likely in one field
Suggested OS map: Explorer 205 Stratford-upon-Avon and Evesham
Parking: on street in Ilmington where possible, Front Street postcode is CV36 4LT
Nearest vet: Avonvale Veterinary Centre, 5 The Rosebird Centre, Shipston Road, Stratford-upon-Avon, CV37 8LU. Tel: 01789 561010

Start point: Front Street, Ilmington OS map: SP214438

Walk 2 Route

Taking the village green as a landmark on Front Street, pass the green on your left and continue to walk down Front Street.

Just after the Shipston-on-Stour T-junction leave Front Street to join a bridleway. This passes a farmhouse on your left and then becomes a green track.

Pass between hedgerows and when the track emerges into a field, turn left to walk around two sides of the field with the hedge on your left.

At the end of the second side, enter the next field and go straight towards a farm house ahead (Berryfield Farm) with woodland to your right. Pass through a metal gate and through the next field (sheep likely here) with a small brook on your right. Go through another metal gate and stay by the brook to cross a further field.

Cross the farm access lane and continue ahead through a gateway. This is a bridleway, and in regular use by horse-riders. Continue ahead in the field with a former railway embankment through the trees to your right.

After just under 400 meters turn right onto a track to leave the field, and pass between the sides of a former railway bridge. You'll soon pass to the right of a small lake.

If your dog enjoys a swim, take a diversion off the track through a small gateway on the left to a lakeside path. Do check that angling isn't underway before letting Fido churn the waters! Then return to the bridleway.

Continue on this peaceful grassy bridleway all the way to Newbold-on-Stour.

At Newbold, reach the Stratford Road and turn left. Pass the village green and cross the road with care to reach The White Hart.

Return to Ilmington

The return route is your outward path in reverse, with the option of adding some variety by taking the path of the old railway.

Cross the road and return to the bridleway, and walk back as far as the old railway bridge.

 Leave the bridleway just before the bridge and turn left to go up the embankment and onto the path of the former railway. Follow to the end, and emerge onto the tarmac farm lane.

Cross over and bear slightly to the right, and then turn left to walk across the field, through a metal gate and through the next field. The brook will be to the left in both these fields.

Continue with the woodland to your left, leaving Berryfield Farm behind you, and into a further field. Keep the hedge to the right, and follow around the field as far as the bridle track on the second side of this field.

Turn right onto the green track and continue ahead to return to Ilmington.

Notes

Walk 3
Willersey and Bretforton

Refreshments: The Bell Inn, Main Street, Willersey, near Broadway WR12 7PJ. Tel: 01386 858405 Opening hours and menus: http://www.thebellwillersey.com

The Bell occupies a handsome 17th century building of Cotswold stone and the food and ales here do justice to their fine surroundings.

Dogs are welcome in the bar, and dog-friendly residential accommodation is also offered.

At the half-way point: The Fleece, Bretforton, Worcs WR11 7JE Tel: 01386 831173. Opening hours and menus: www.thefleeceinn.co.uk

Astonishingly, The Fleece Inn dates back to the early 15th century which makes the building just a bit special. It's now owned by the National Trust – and hosts a number of traditional events, such as the asparagus festival, Morris dancing, live music and exhibitions in the adjacent barn.

A glass of locally produced apple juice or cider at The Fleece is just right for this half-way point of your walk. The Fleece is dog-friendly.

Walk map

Walk info

A completely hill-free circular walk over fertile fields of the Vale of Evesham, with a charming National Trust thatched inn and medieval village at the half-way point

Length: 6.5 miles (10.5km)
Stiles: 6
Livestock: cows likely in 3 fields, with separated footpath
Suggested OS map: Explorer 205 Stratford-upon-Avon & Evesham, and OL45 The Cotswolds
Parking: on street in Willersey, or The Bell car park if you're taking refreshment. WR12 7PJ
Nearest vet: Avonvale Veterinary Centre, 5 The Rosebird Centre, Shipston Road, Stratford-upon-Avon, CV37 8LU Tel: 01789 561010

Start point: The Bell Inn, Willersey OS map: SP105397

Walk 3 Route

With your back to The Bell turn right and walk down Main Street through the village.

At the mini-roundabout, turn left and cross the road and after a few paces turn right at a footpath sign leading you across the recreation ground to its far left corner.

Take the narrow path here to pass behind a few houses with a small brook to the left. Turn left onto a residential street, cross the brook and continue past a group of executive homes. Follow the footpath ahead and you'll shortly find yourself on a somewhat overgrown former railway track.

Go straight ahead, off the old railway track, passing a yellow waymarker on the left, and follow the narrow pathway round to the left and alongside a field to go over a stile. Dogs can easily pass underneath.

This short section of path may be almost choked with vegetation (despite the efforts of local walkers to lop the greenery back) and many walkers step over the wire fence to walk in the adjacent field. If you have secateurs in your backpack, this may be their moment of glory.

From the stile turn left, past a small orchard and a knee-high waymarker post.

Walk straight across the field to reach a British Opencast Coal waymarker to the left of a telegraph post. Turn right, and then left at the telegraph post and continue to the far side of the field ahead.

Cross over two footbridges and turn right in the field.

Continue with the brook always on your right over a succession of six fields. The crops vary from broad beans, cereals and rape according to season and the changing colours and scents attract many different types of butterfly and other insects.

Cross the access drive to Downrip Farm at the end of field 5, and go over a dilapidated stile into field 6.

Just before the end of this field, go through a metal farm gate on the right and pass to the left of a magnificent oak tree towards and then over a wooden stile giving access onto a country lane. This stile may be awkward for dogs unwilling to tackle a gap under the hedge on the right.

Turn left on the lane and after a few paces turn right by a cattle grid onto a bridleway, which is also a long driveway to Willersey Barn.

When the driveway bears right towards the house, continue straight ahead with a hedge to your right.

Pass through a kissing gate and turn right in the field and then left along the field edge with a ditch to the right.

Cross a plank bridge and through another kissing gate into the next field. Go through a farm gate at the end of this field and turn left onto a track.

After a few paces turn right at a footpath post and into a grassy field, walking with the hedge and brook (a ditch in dry weather) on your right. You'll see a cluster of barns over on the left.

15

Cross a tractor bridge into the next field, bear right and walk with the hedge to your right. Go through a metal gate at the end of the field and continue ahead across a final field towards a gabled house ahead. Go through the gate and turn right on the lane. There's a dog waste bin on the left.

To reach The Fleece Inn and the village centre turn left onto Bridge Street. At the church turn right and the inn is in front of you. To continue the walk, return to the bridge and turn left.

Return to Willersey

Continue along the lane until it bends around to the right, ignoring one footpath sign to the left. At the bend go straight on and through a kissing gate to enter a paddock and go straight ahead. Notice the brook to the left – this will stay with you for the following 3 miles.

Go through a metal gate and walk with the hedge on the left through field 1. Go through a kissing gate and pass through a copse to enter field 2 over a stile, with plenty of space for dogs to go underneath, and continue with the brook to the left.

Pass through a metal kissing gate and carry on, passing a market garden on the right. There's a dog waste bin at the end of this field.

Cross a narrow lane and metal kissing gate to enter field 3. Stay in the same direction to go through a metal gate into field 4. Continue ahead in field 5, where the brook is still to your left, and then into field 6. Enter field 7 through a metal gate, pass through a copse and turn left. Take a wooden gate into field 8.

Continue straight, passing first a solar farm and then mounds of earthworks on the right, as far as a broad track on the left which runs through a silver birch wood.

Turn left onto this track, cross over the brook and immediately turn right on a little trodden path.

Follow this path left around the trees and then turn right to cross the brook again on a wooden footbridge and enter field 9.

Turn left in this field, walking with the woodland and hedge to the left, and go over a footbridge into field 10 where the pointy spire of the church in Saintbury will be directly ahead.

Cross this field and go over a low stile into field 11 and continue in the same direction to the far side of the field and walk up a small embankment to join the old railway line.

Turn right onto the old railway and continue ahead, crossing the Badsey road on a bridge and then to the rear of houses in Willersey until you reach the path crossroads from the start of the walk.

Turn left here, and retrace your steps to cross the recreation ground and return to the Bell Inn.

Notes

Walk 4
Cleeve Prior

Refreshments: The King's Arms, Cleeve Road, Cleeve Prior, Worcs, WR11 8LQ. Tel: 01789 773335 Opening hours and menus: www.cleeveprior.org.uk/kings.html

On the way into the Kings Arms, do notice the building next door, a former cider brewery – surely a sign that this part of the village has a long tradition of quenching thirsts.

This is a friendly and welcoming pub, serving reliable pub favourites and a fine roast on Sundays. Dogs are welcome in the bar area and at the outside tables.

The small car park is for patrons only, but there's also plenty of on-street parking on the road nearby.

Walk map

Walk info

A visit to the village of Cleeve Prior is close to a time-travel experience, with the chance to see a number of fantastically old houses and farm buildings looking much as they did many centuries ago. Records show that Cleeve Prior has been a prosperous rural village for nearly a thousand years, and its quiet understated charm is best appreciated on foot.

Length: 5.25 miles (8.4km)
Stiles: 6 (all but one with dog holes)
Livestock: possible in nature reserve
Suggested OS map: Explorer 205 Stratford-upon-Avon & Evesham
Parking: In the Kings Arms car park (WR11 8LQ) if you're taking refreshment, otherwise on street.
Nearest vet: Avonvale Veterinary Centre, 5 The Rosebird Centre, Shipston Road, Stratford-upon-Avon, CV37 8LU Tel: 01789 561010

Start Point: in front of the King's Arms OS map: SP089493

Walk 4 Route

With your back to the King's Arms turn left and walk on the Main Street pavement. Cross the stile on the left, entering a recreation field by the school. Cross the field with a children's playground to the left and go through a metal kissing gate ahead.

Go straight across the field to the fence and trees ahead, with horse paddocks to your left.

Go over a stile and walk through a small orchard.

Then turn left onto a farm track, with a ditch to your right. Ignore all footpath signs to the right and left and keep forward on the track.

Pass a Severn Trent water structure on the left, and continue forward into an arable field. Electric cables will be just on the left to start with.

Stay in the same direction to the end of the field, then take a few paces to the right and cross a footbridge and stile into the next field. Most dogs will easily pass under the stile.

Continue ahead, with a fence and small ditch to the right. Ignore a footpath going off to the right and carry on to the end of the field. Stay in the same direction, and go through a metal gate to walk across a further field.

Cross a small stile with large dog gap at the far side and walk on a fenced path between a field on the right and paddocks on the left. The rooftops of North Littleton are visible over on the left.

Stay in the same direction, ignoring a stile and footpath marker leading off to the left. Pass through a metal kissing gate, with dog waste bin, and cross the road.

Continue on the footpath to the left of 'Inglenook'. The hedge will be on your right. Ahead you'll be able to see the church tower of Middle Littleton. Pass through a metal kissing gate and turn left. The gorgeous old building ahead is the Tithe Barn of Middle Littleton, a National Trust property.

A detour to see more of the Tithe Barn is worthwhile, so go through the kissing gate on the left and immediately turn left on the track to reach it.

Return to the field and turn left. Go through a kissing gate into a further field, with houses to the left. At the end of the field cross the road and continue straight on through a kissing gate to the left of 'Edenbrook'.

Keep the post and rail fence to the right, and enter another field through a metal gate.

Keep in the same direction to reach a further metal gate, and a fantastic view of the Avon plain below.

Head down the steep slope and through a metal kissing gate at the bottom and go forward in the field to exit by the side of a stile opposite the Offenham Park static caravan site. Cross the road with care, enter the caravan site and continue on a cinder track to a field on the far side. The river Avon will be on your left.

You're now walking on the 'Shakespeare's Way', a long distance path which follows the full length of the river Avon. Much of the path has been eroded, and you'll pass a number of redundant stiles which may well have the river lapping underneath.

Just after a weir in the river the track comes to an end. Walk between two wooden chalets and cross a double stile and bridge combo.

Keep the river to the left and walk through a young plantation, over a final stile and into a grazing field. Continue over the next field and stick to the river path over more fields. Pass Stubbs Pool fishery to the right.

The path narrows and then forks at the start of woodland. Take the right hand fork up an incline and walk through the trees with the river falling away to the left. You'll emerge in a grassy clearing where the footpath meets a bridleway.

Turn left on the bridleway and keep going, crossing a single-track lane and then a bungalow 'Hillside' on the left. At a wooden gate continue on the shaded bridleway.

Pass a house on the left, and then turn right a few paces after a chain fence to pass through some sturdy metal posts and join a footpath crossing an arable field. Continue straight, passing allotments to the left. Cross an unsurfaced lane and take the footpath to the right of a metal farm gate.

Go through a metal kissing gate and turn left, with the hedge now to the left. Pass through another kissing gate and continue in the same direction.

After the next kissing gate, enter a larger field (often with placid horses) and turn right. Cross a plank footbridge and another kissing gate to walk down the left side of the next field. Notice Cleeve Manor to your left. The path leads into the churchyard.

Pass the church to your right and continue forward to join a shared driveway leading to the road and the Kings Arms.

Notes

Walk 5
Barton to Cleeve Prior

Refreshments: The Cottage of Content, 15 Welford Road, Barton, near Bidford on Avon, Warwickshire B50 4NP. Tel: 01789 772279. Opening hours and menus: www.cottageofcontent.com

The Cottage of Content is a genuinely old pub, surrounded by thatched cottages and close to the River Avon. Their menu is ideal for hungry walkers, and it's a popular establishment.

Camping is possible on a field behind the pub in summer. Dogs are welcome in the bar and at the garden tables.

Walk map

Walk info

This walk passes by Bidford-on-Avon, a village with a long history, due to its position as a safe place to ford the River Avon.

Legend has it that William Shakespeare took part in a drinking competition in Bidford and eventually passed out under a crab apple tree. When his drinking chums wanted to extend the binge, Shakespeare reputedly said: "No. I have drunk with "Piping Pebworth, Dancing Marston, Haunted Hillboro', Hungry Grafton, Dodging Exhall, Papist Wixford, Beggarly Broom and Drunken Bidford" and so, presumably, I will drink no more." It's unlikely to be true, but there always have been a lot of pubs in Bidford!

Length: 5.4 miles (8.6km)
Stiles: 3
Livestock: sheep likely in one field
Suggested OS map: Explorer 205 Stratford-upon-Avon & Evesham
Parking: Cottage of Content, B50 4NP
Public WC: Bidford Recreation ground
Nearest vet: Avonvale Veterinary Centre, 5 The Rosebird Centre, Shipston Road, Stratford-upon-Avon, CV37 8LU Tel: 01789 561010

Start point: Cottage of Content, Barton OS map: SP107512

Walk 5 Route

Turn left from the Cottage of Content onto an unsurfaced track. Bear left after a caravan park on a footpath with the river Avon on your right. Emerge into a field (sheep likely) and cross this field and the next, heading towards the medieval bridge at Bidford.

Cross the road and enter Bidford recreation ground, and continue to walk on a riverside path with the Avon on your right. There are a number of dog waste bins here. When the broad path runs out continue ahead into a field, signed the Avon River Walk. Go straight on through four fields with the river always just on the right.

Cross a wooden footbridge after the fourth field and you'll see a walkers' signpost. Turn left here towards Marlcliff on a stony track and continue past a well-tended garden to a wooden gate on the right just before Bramble Cottage.

Turn right through the gate, marked with several footpath arrows.

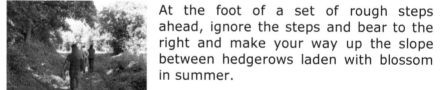

At the foot of a set of rough steps ahead, ignore the steps and bear to the right and make your way up the slope between hedgerows laden with blossom in summer.

You'll pass a wooden bench on the left, ideally placed for a view and a breather. Then go through a couple of metal gates, following the Shakespeare's Avon Way footpath arrow.

From the top of the ridge, do pause to enjoy the view of the Avon and the fields over towards Bidford. Continue to follow the Avon Way along a clear footpath that runs between fields and follows the line of the River Avon. There are horse training tracks to the right.

Cross a wide farm track leading off to the left, and carry straight on. You'll soon be able to see the houses of Cleeve Prior over to the left.

Just before you reach a white cottage (Cleeve House) with a single chain fence, turn left into a field passing through a set of upright metal posts. This path is unsigned, so don't be tempted by the footpath arrows leading past the house.

Go straight on at the footpath crossings at the end of the field. This is a farm track. Cross over a bridleway/track at the next 'crossing' and along a narrow pathway into a field.

Go through a kissing gate at the end of the field and turn left. The hedgerow will be on your left here.

At the end of this field go through another kissing gate, and then continue to follow the path across one more field and kissing gate.

Now turn left, marked with a yellow footpath arrow, and walk to the end of this field and through another kissing gate. Go straight on here, through an arable field with the hedge on the left.

At the next kissing gate carry on, the hedge will now be to the right, and follow the path as it curls around the bottom corner of the field and through an old gateway two-thirds up, and into the next field.

Pass the apple trees of an old orchard and across a small field to go over a rustic wooden stile (there's a gap for dogs to get through).

Head for the far left corner of the next field and go straight on over the stile (which also has a dog gap). Don't be waylaid by a footpath sign and stile on the left hand side. Start heading downhill to go over another stile with a dog gap and then keep going straight on the footpath.

Go down the steps and straight on through the wooden gate to reach the lane in Marlcliff. Turn left, and retrace your route down the unsurfaced lane to the river.

Turn right at the waymarker sign, walking towards Bidford over the fields with the river to the left.

Walk on the path through the recreation ground, and cross the road at the bridge. Cross the fields and return to the Cottage of Content.

Walk 6
Barton and Collett's Wood

Walk map

A second walk from Barton, this time towards the hamlet of Dorsington. The late Felix Dennis, publisher, playboy and poet, was a resident of Dorsington. He was the driving force behind the Heart of England Forest project and his financial legacy continues to support the development of the new forest. This walk goes through several of the new woodlands, and the pool in Collett's Wood is a delightful spot for contemplation.

Walk info

Refreshments: The Cottage of Content, 15 Welford Road, Barton, near Bidford on Avon, Warwickshire B50 4NP. Tel: 01789 772279. Opening hours and menus: www.cottageofcontent.com

Length: 3.7 miles (6km)
Stiles: 1 (with dog gate)
Livestock: sheep likely by Collets Farm
Suggested OS map: Explorer 205 Stratford-upon-Avon & Evesham
Parking: The Cottage of Content car park if taking refreshment, or on street in village
Nearest vet: Avonvale Veterinary Centre, 5 The Rosebird Centre, Shipston Road, Stratford-upon-Avon, CV37 8LU Tel: 01789 561010

Start point: The Cottage of Content, Barton OS map: SP107512

Walk 6 Route

From the Cottage of Content, turn right onto the road. As the road bends to the right, take a left turn to pass Owlets End and carry on down the lane, Heart of England Way. Off-lead dogs are fine on this track – cars/farm vehicles use it for access only.

Continue until you see Barton Hill House.

Turn right just before Barton Hill House to stay on the Heart of England Way. The path makes its way along the left hand side of the field, heading down the slope with the hedge to the left. At the end of the field, go through the large gap and turn left. The hedge will still be on your left.

At the end of the field, pass through the gap into another field. Keep to the left hand side of this field with the hedge on the left.

Go through the large gap ahead and then turn right at a Heart of England Way arrow to walk down the next field with the hedge on your right. Go straight on at the end of the field to pass through a copse of trees.

Go through a wooden gate and follow the path as it skirts around Collett's Wood. On the left there's a large pond and benches where you can sit and watch dragonflies enjoying the water

Continue straight with the hedge on the right and go over the stile with dog gate by a 5-bar wooden gate. The gate can usually be opened for large dogs.

Go straight on in the next field with the hedge still on the right. Collett's Farm can be seen to the left.

Go through a 5-bar wooden gate at the end of the field and turn right onto the farm track. After a few paces, bear left to follow a blue bridlepath arrow.

Keep to this bridleway ignoring one turn to the left, and passing a 5-bar wooden gate (number 20). The hedgeline will always be on your left.

The path emerges onto an unsurfaced farm track. Turn right here and continue past a cottage on your right. Go through the 5-bar wooden gate to stay on the farm track with woodland (Fox Covert) on the left.

As the track bears left, look for a plank bridge and stile on the right. Cross over the stile and walk along the right side of the field. Turn left at the far side to reach a metal footbridge in the corner.

If the stile is too overgrown to use, a solution is to enter the same field

through an open gateway on the right a little further on and then keep to the left hand side of the field to reach the metal footbridge at the far corner. This is not the correct footpath, despite being more trodden.

Cross the footbridge, and carry straight on in the next field, keeping the hedge on the right.

After 400m, at a denser collection of trees on the right, turn right to go over a wooden footbridge. In summer this can be hard to spot.

Follow the path along the left hand side of the field, keeping the trees to the left. The footpath now goes over a footbridge and through the woodland. At times this path may be so overgrown with brambles that it's impenetrable. An option used by many ramblers is to stay in the field and walk to the end of the trees, a diversion of 60m from the legal footpath.

Turn right onto the farm track which crosses the middle of the field.

Stay on this track as it bends left into the next field and carry straight on through the trees. Ignore a track to the right which appears almost immediately.

On entering a field, turn left. Keep the hedge on your left and pass a converted barn also on the left.

Follow the track to a T-junction, where you turn left and re-join your outward route. Turn right at the road and return to the Cottage of Content.

Notes

Walk 7
Wixford and Oversley Wood

Refreshments: The Fish Inn, Wixford, Warks, B49 6DA. Tel: 01789 778593. Opening hours and menus: www.thefishatwixford.com

Quirky, fun and stylish describes the inside of The Fish, where Spider the pub dog keeps a mischievous eye on the large outdoor beer garden next to the River Arrow. There's lots of outdoor space, with play spaces for kids and easy access to the river for doggie swimming.

Sandwiches and full meals are available, and these are tasty and well-presented.

Dogs are welcome in the bar, and in the enormous beer garden.

Walk map

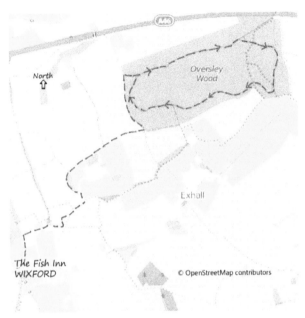

Walk info

Wixford is a tiny village nestled on the bank of the River Arrow. The walk passes the church of St Milburga of Wenlock, a little known Saxon saint who was an eighth century abbess.

Length: 5.5 miles (8.8km)
Stiles: 0
Livestock: 0
Suggested OS map: Explorer 205 Stratford-upon-Avon & Evesham
Parking: The Fish overflow car park, B49 6DA
Nearest vet: Severn Veterinary Centre, 1 Cross Road, Alcester, B49 5EX. Tel: 01789 764455

Start point: The Fish Inn, Wixford OS map: SP088545

Walk 7 Route

From the Fish Inn, walk across the car park to join a track passing a small caravan park on your left. Do pause to admire the inventive display of ornamental gnomes and friends in the last garden. Continue ahead through two metal kissing gates.

When the path splits, bear right on the Heart of England Way.

Continue ahead, passing St Milburga's church on your left.

Carry straight on at the track crossroads, up a private access lane and public footpath to the side of the wrought iron gate.

Pass through a kissing gate and turn left to continue along the lane, around several bends and gently uphill. The mock castellations of Oversley Castle can be seen on the hilltop. On reaching the gateway marked private, turn left on the Heart of England Way along a track with the hedge on your right.

At the track T-junction turn right on the Heart of England Way. Pass Castle Cottage on your left, and have dogs on leads here because of free-range hens.

When the track forks soon after, bear right (not the Heart of England Way) heading towards Oversley Wood.

At the corner of the woodland look for a waymarker post covered in direction arrows just a few steps into the woodland. Turn left, taking the direction of a bridleway, and walking with the wood on your right.

Continue down the grassy track as far as a surfaced path and turn right here to enter the wood.

At the path T-junction turn left. There is a deep carpet of bluebells here in the spring.

Follow the undulating path, ignoring all minor paths to the right and left, to a large fork in the track. Take the right hand fork and carry on around the woodland on this circular path.

After just under 2 miles you'll return to the point where you entered the woods.

Turn left, and then left again on the bridleway track to retrace your route back to Wixford.

Notes

Walk 8
Stratford to Clifford Chambers

Refreshments: Marina Café Bistro, Stratford Marina, Bridgeway, Stratford upon Avon, Warwickshire CV37 6YY. Tel: 01789 299921 Opening hours and menu: www.marinacafebistrostratford.co.uk

The Marina Café Bistro is well off the busy tourist track and has the advantage of an excellent riverside view, together with a large carpark nearby offering the most reasonably priced parking in the town.

The food has a Spanish influence, and in warm weather a meal on the terrace becomes a Mediterranean delight.

Children and dogs welcome.

Walk map

Walk info

Stratford is known all over the world as the birthplace of Shakespeare. This walk gives fine views of the theatre and Holy Trinity church where Shakespeare is buried, and onward to the quiet hamlet of Clifford Chambers. The circular route takes in some lesser known sights and sounds of the Stour Valley to the south of the town.

Length: 6.5 miles (10.7km).
Stiles: 1
Livestock: unlikely
Suggested OS map: Explorer 205 Stratford-upon-Avon & Evesham
Parking: Marina car park (CV37 6YY) – all day charge, or other long-stay car parks in the town
Public WCs: Stratford Rec
Nearest vet: Avonvale Veterinary Centre, 5 The Rosebird Centre, Shipston Road, Stratford-upon-Avon, CV37 8LU Tel: 01789 561010

Start point: the Butterfly Farm, well signed from the Avon Pleasure Gardens. OS Map: SP205547

Walk 8 Route

Pass the entrance to the Butterfly Farm, and continue for half-a-mile on the hard-surfaced raised walkway to its end. In the early 19th century this was a horse-drawn tram route from Stratford to Moreton-in-Marsh.

Cross the road ahead at the end. Follow the footpath around the junction and then turn right to walk on the Mickleton road pavement for just under 200m.

Cross the road with care and turn left over a stile - alas, no dog gate on this one but the gap is quite generous.

Follow the line of the footpath through the middle of the field, in the direction of the footpath arrow. It's a well-used path and easy to see.

Over on the far side of the field keep the hedge to the left and follow it around a corner.

The path then runs by a fence, and becomes a track running through the centre of two large fields. Head straight on towards a group of farm buildings, now a small business centre. Pass the first barn to the left, then bear left on the track between the barns to a wire fence ahead.

On the corner post you'll see footpath arrows. Turn right and head slightly downhill - all the barns will now be over on your right.

Go along the track and then turn left at a waymarked gate towards the village of Clifford Chambers. There may be livestock in the field, and the path has been fenced so that walkers are safely separated from cows.

In the next field, bear half-right towards the trees after the kissing gate.

Cross the footbridge over the river Stour. Pass a house on the left and carry on into Clifford Chambers.

The village is very old, and the rectory has a claim to be the 'real' birthplace of Shakespeare; had his mother been concerned about an outbreak of plague in Stratford this was the regular refuge for well-to-do townsfolk.

Walk the length of the main street, the manor house is worth a quick peep through the big iron gates, as far as a pub.

Cross the road and pass a pinfold on the left. There's a board explaining what it was used for, but the gate is firmly locked against a closer look.

Ignore the road turning to the left, and look out for a bridleway marker in the hedge just around the bend on Clifford Lane. Follow the long, straight bridleway past a farm cottage on the left and forward between several fields.

Eventually the bridleway meets the Greenway where you turn right towards Stratford. It's a multi-user path, so don't be surprised by cyclists and joggers.

Just before a chunky but old and rusting metal railway bridge take a footpath signed to the right. This leads down the embankment to a gate. Turn sharp left here.

The path now follows the river, with fields of vegetables on the right. Stay on the river path, passing a lock and then going under the road to return to the pleasure gardens.

The bustle of the town is suddenly around you again. To reach the Dirty Duck for refreshments, take the chain ferry across the river; or pass by the theatre and bear right to return to the Marina Bistro.

Walk 9
Stratford - River Avon walk

Refreshments: Carriages Café, Greenway car park. Opening hours chalked up, mainly weekends but other days too in school holidays. WCs, 50p charge if not a customer.

Alternative refreshments at the Dirty Duck, Waterside, Stratford-upon-Avon CV37 6BA. Tel: 01789 297312. Menu: https://www.oldenglishinns.co.uk/our-locations/the-dirty-duck-stratford-upon-avon. Dog-friendly in the bar and garden.

Walk map

Walk info

This is a gentle riverside walk with views over to Holy Trinity church and the Old Town of Stratford-upon-Avon. It is impossible to think that Shakespeare would not have wandered through the meadows here.

Length: 4.3 miles (7km)
Stiles: 0
Livestock: sheep possible in one field
Suggested OS map: Explorer 205 Stratford-upon-Avon & Evesham
Parking: Greenway free car park, Seven Meadows Road, Stratford-upon-Avon CV37 6GR
Nearest vet: Avonvale Veterinary Centre, 5 The Rosebird Centre, Shipston Road, Stratford-upon-Avon, CV37 8LU Tel: 01789 561010
Waste bin: Greenway car park

Start: Greenway car park, Seven Meadows Road, Stratford-upon-Avon.

Walk 9 Route

Leave the car park and walk towards the Greenway. Almost immediately (and before the converted railway carriages) turn right to walk on a shaded path through the hedge, over a stream and past the back of houses to the right, and enter the racecourse through a metal kissing gate.

Duck under the railings and cross the race track on the public footpath, then go through the wooden gate. Carry straight on, passing the grandstand over to your right. Join a short track and go through another wooden gate. Keep going to walk along a hedge-lined path.

Go under the railings and across the race track, then through a metal kissing gate and immediately turn left.

This path lies next to the racecourse and emerges into a grassy field. Continue straight on with the racecourse still on your left.

At the corner of the field, by the old railway bridge over the River Avon, turn left to go over a footbridge and through a metal kissing gate.

Follow the path as it makes its way under the arches of the railway bridge. The river will be on your right.

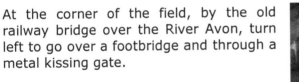

Follow the riverside path (Monarch's Way) towards Stratford-upon-Avon. This section is a delight for dogs who love to swim, and a great place too for just sitting by the river and enjoying the riverbank.

In the field after crossing a wooden footbridge, look diagonally across to the left to spot the spire of Holy Trinity Church in the distance, where William Shakespeare is buried. It's not at all fanciful to imagine the poet walking along this riverbank noticing the wild flowers that gave inspiration to famous lines such as these, from A Midsummer Night's Dream:

I know a bank where the wild thyme blows, Where oxlips and the nodding violet grows,
Quite over-canopied with luscious woodbine, With sweet musk-roses and with eglantine...

As the river path approaches Stratford, pass a lock and weir on the river and then walk beneath the road bridge. Turn right to cross the Avon on the footbridge (dog waste bins here) with a view of the pleasure gardens.

On the far bank, turn right to walk back under the road. Go through a wooden kissing gate and again enjoy the river path with the Avon now on your right. The path is signed for the Milcote Picnic area.

When you reach a lock, bear left following the clearly signed path up the steps to a shaded path between fields and the higher banks of the river.

After 400m, descend again to the river. At the end of some steps, cross a plank bridge and stay with the path through three metal gates and into a field. Stay in the same direction, keeping the river on the right over this field and the next.

When the old railway bridge comes into view continue along the edge of the field as far as a metal kissing gate. Go through this and then turn right through a metal gate to head up the embankment and rejoin the Greenway. Bear right onto the Greenway and cross over the old railway bridge (dog waste bin on the right) and return to the car park.

Notes

Walk 10
Kings Coughton

Refreshments: The Twisted Boot, Birmingham Road, Kings Coughton, Warks B49 5QF. Tel: 01789 763111. Opening hours and menus: http://www.kingscourthotel.co.uk/dining/the-twisted-boot-bar.html

The Twisted Boot is part of the Kings Court Hotel, and is thoroughly welcoming to walkers – and their dogs. You'll find a terrific buffet lunch during the week, with diners in the bar and garden enjoying the same high quality food as those in the dining room. Sunday lunches are also great value, and very popular, so booking ahead is a good idea.

Walk map

Walk info

A highly enjoyable walk, largely through young plantations of the Heart of England forest project and farmland. On a clear day the view of wildflower-strewn meadows is a joy.

Length: 5.5 miles (8.8km)
Stiles: none
Livestock: sheep possible in 2 or 3 fields
Suggested OS map: Explorer 220 Birmingham, and Explorer 205 Stratford-upon-Avon & Evesham
Parking: The Kings Court Hotel car park B49 5QF
Nearest vet: Severn Veterinary Centre, 1 Cross Road, Alcester, B49 5EX Tel: 01789 764455

Start point: The Kings Court Hotel. OS map: SP083592

Walk 10 Route

Leave the hotel car park and turn left on an access lane to the side of the hotel. Turn left onto a public footpath opposite a caravan storage field.

Walk along the left side of the field with a hedge and brook to your left.

Turn right at the far end and after 150 meters go through a metal gate on the left to enter the next field. You'll now be able to see the spire of Coughton church ahead.

Walk along the left side of this field, pass through a gate at the far side and continue ahead through a further field (sheep likely) and through a gate to reach Coughton Fields lane, opposite the entrance to the Coughton Court coach park.

Turn right on the lane and cross the River Arrow using the footbridge to the side of Coughton ford. Turn left just after the ford to join an unclassified county road/Arden Way.

Walk along the track for 600 meters, ignoring a pair of kissing gates to left and right, towards a small hill – Windmill Hill.

Just after a group of three metal farm gates turn left through a metal kissing gate. Walk forward, past a single oak tree to the left and through a further metal gate. This short section of path can get very over-grown but don't be put off.

Continue, with a high deer-proof fence to the left. Windmill Hill will now be to the right.

Go through a gate in the high fence and continue ahead with the hedge on the right, heading towards a farm. You're now walking in the Heart of England Forest project, where young trees are at the start of their lives and will eventually turn these fields into mature woodland.

At the bottom of the young plantation cross a wooden farm bridge and continue on a farm track towards Middle Spernall Farm with the hedge to the right.

Go through a metal gate in the high wire fence and pass through the farm buildings and through the gate to the side of a cattle grid. Follow the footpath as far as the end of the field.

Stay in the field (sheep are likely here) and turn left, passing a kissing gate on the right. Now keep the hedgerow to your right and after 200m turn right and pass through two metal gates, into more of the Heart of England Forest.

Bear ahead and slightly left on the grassy path and head down the slope to cross a plank footbridge.

Now continue up the slope ahead, aiming at the copse of mature trees ahead.

Go through a hard-to-spot gap in the hedge and into the copse, and out the other side.

Take a few paces to the right, and then turn left on a little-trodden path. You may spot a white footpath arrow along the way for reassurance.

Turn left through a metal gate with footpath markers, very well hidden behind an oak tree. At the time of writing there's also a square wooden arch to mark the place to turn left.

Walk ahead with saplings to your right.

Continue straight across the next field, where Lower Spernall Farm will be visible on the left.

Cross the farm access track and through a kissing gate directly ahead.

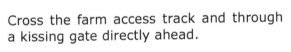

Turn left and walk with the stock fence to your left, around the farm and go through a wooden gate to the left of the River Arrow.

Continue through two more metal gates with the river on the right.

Cross a wooden footbridge and walk ahead through the young plantation.

Cross a further footbridge and walk with the hedge to your right, and the river too. Go over another plank bridge and keep going to a metal kissing gate ahead, next to a National Trust post.

You're now in the Coughton Estate, where the young saplings give way to grassy parkland and mature oaks. Pass Timm's Grove to the left, and follow the footpath past a line of mature oaks to your left with Coughton Court ahead and to the right.

A diversion to the left into Timm's Grove is well worthwhile, especially at bluebell time. This is possibly a survivor of very ancient woodland, and you'll find an interpretation board conveniently placed near the wooden entry gate.

When the river re-appears ahead, turn left into a marshy field and then go through a kissing gate at the far side. These fields are popular with herons, and you may see several of them feasting on frogs and tasty field-fare.

Go straight across the track and through a further kissing gate directly ahead.

Keep ahead in the field and through a kissing gate to reach the next field.

Continue ahead with the river to the right. At the far side of the field, turn right (there's a hard to spot, knee-high footpath marker) and go through a metal gate onto Coughton Fields Lane. Turn left.

Just before Millford House turn right at the public footpath marker and cross the river on a footbridge. Go straight across the field (sheep likely) and through a metal kissing gate into a further field. Coughton Court will be to your right.

Bear left to walk along the left side of the field (sheep) and turn left at the gate.

You're now retracing the outward route, walking straight across the fields and parallel to the Birmingham Road as far as the caravans. Turn right onto the service lane and return to the Twisted Boot.

Notes

Walk 11
Coughton

Refreshments: The Throckmorton Arms, Coughton Hill, Alcester, Warks B49 5HX. Tel: 01789 766366 Opening hours and menus: www.thethrockmorton.com

The Throckmorton Arms, named after the family who have owned nearby Coughton Court for the last six centuries, is perfectly placed for the start of an interesting and varied walk. Afterwards, a log fire burns in winter and on warmer days a large outside terrace is perfect for dog-walkers.

Dogs are welcome in the bar and on the terrace.

Walk map

Walk info

An easy-going walk over fields and young forest plantations, with access to the river for dog swimming.

Length: 5.7 miles (9km)
Stiles: 0
Livestock: sheep likely in 2 or 3 fields
Suggested OS map: Explorer 220 Birmingham
Parking: Throckmorton Arms car park (with permission)
Nearest vet: Severn Veterinary Centre, 1 Cross Road, Alcester, B49 5EX Tel: 01789 764455

Start point: The Throckmorton Arms OS map: SP079609

Walk 11 Route

From the Throckmorton Arms car park, walk down the field towards a metal gate.

Go through and cross the footbridge, then turn left to walk with the stream on your left through a couple of walkers' gates and up to the road at the bridge.

Turn left, cross the road with care, then walk through the gateposts by a red brick house. Go through the metal kissing gate ahead into National Trust grounds and head diagonally left to reach the far left corner of the field.

Go through the kissing gate and carry on in the next field with a metal fence on your left.

After 30m, go through another metal kissing gate and turn left in the next field. Walk over this field with a hedge on the left and telephone wires above on the right.

Turn right at the end of the field. After 40m, turn left and go through a metal gate on your right.

Bear slightly right in the next large field, walking across the middle of the field and aiming towards the trees ahead. Eventually you will be able to spot a walkers' gate on the far side. If you're with a dog who loves swimming, there's a natural river pool to the right of the gate with easy access to the water.

Go through the gate and walk with the river on your right. On the left you'll see a plantation of young trees and this is part of the Heart of England Forest project.

Cross over the footbridge at the end of the field and continue ahead. This path passes to the right of a small church.

Go through a wooden gate, bear left on a farm access track and follow this for a short distance to reach a country lane. Turn right onto the lane.

Pass one house on the left, then turn left at a Millennium Way footpath marker through a metal kissing gate, then through another metal gate and take the constrained footpath heading uphill. This can get unpleasantly overgrown in summer, but at least it's a short section.

After a metal gate the path opens out. Continue uphill with the hedge on your left. Go straight through another gate into the next field. This is still part of the new forest project, and paths have been mowed which don't match the public footpath which can be confusing.

Walk to the left hand side of the telegraph poles. You should be able to spot a yellow footpath arrow on the side. Head gently downhill and continue with the hedgerow on your left to reach the driveway to a red brick farmhouse.

Go through the wooden gate which takes you along the side of the farmhouse garden. Leave the garden at a wooden gate ahead and continue in the same direction in the next field with the ditch and hedge on your right.

At the end of the field, turn left to go through a gateway into another field. Walk around the right hand side of the field (sheep likely here) following the stream.

At the end of this field, go through the metal kissing gate and turn right onto a farm track and follow this past the Unipart Wood on the right and onward as far as a gate marked 'nature reserve'.

Now bear left to enter a new plantation field. There's a faint fork in the path here. Take the left fork and aim to pass the central group of trees to your right.

Keep going towards the church. The path will become constrained and passes through a wooden gate into a cemetery. Continue ahead and through a wooden gate onto a lane opposite the church building (dog waste bin by gate).

Turn left on the lane. At the corner, carry straight on through the metal kissing gate into a field.

Follow the well-trodden path with the river to the right. There are a few small beaches, ideal for dog splashing and drinking.

At the end of this large field, go through a metal gate and turn left. A hedge will be on your left.

At the end of the field go through a metal kissing gate, over the footbridge, and bear right to reach a metal gate ahead signed the Arden Way.

Carry straight on through a few gates, past a farm and then a group of barn conversions on the left, and walk down their access lane (with cattle grids) to reach Spernal Lane again.

Turn left, and then take the first right turn to pass the vicarage and church to the right. You are now back on your outward route

Cross over the footbridge ahead and keep ahead until you can see Coughton Court. Turn right when Coughton Court is just across a field and head for the red-brick house to cross the busy road again.

The little stream on the way back to the Throckmorton Arms is ideal for a paw and wellie wash on muddy days.

Walk 12
Great Alne

Refreshments: The Mother Huff Cap, Spernall Lane, Great Alne, B49 6HY. Tel: 01789 488800. Opening hours and menus: www.facebook.com/themotherhuffcap2015

The Mother Huff Cap has been a pub for some 400 years, and it's thought that the unusual name could be associated with a strong alcoholic cider (perry) made from local pears, as several heritage pear varieties are known as yellow, black or red huff caps.

The menu has meals to suit all appetites and pockets, with fixed price meal deals popular with families.

Dogs are welcome in the special 'dog lounge' at the rear, and at the outside tables.

Walk map

Walk info

A thoroughly rural walk over fields criss-crossed with small streams and hedgerows full of wild fruits and birds' nests.

Length: 4 miles (6.4km)
Stiles: none
Livestock: cows possible in one field. Horses probable in several fields, with a taped-off footpath route.
Suggested OS map: Explorer 205 Stratford-upon-Avon & Evesham, and Explorer 220 Birmingham
Parking: Mother Huff Cap car park B49 6HY (with permission)
Nearest vet: Severn Veterinary Centre, 1 Cross Road, Alcester, B49 5EX Tel: 01789 764455
Waste bins: at start of walk

Start point: Mother Huff Cap OS map: SP113593

Walk 12 Route

Leave the pub car park and turn left onto Spernal Lane. After a few yards cross the road and turn right onto a signed public footpath, by a dog waste bin.

Walk across the field with a hedge to your left.

Enter the next field and continue in the same direction, passing a tennis court on the right.

Walk round two sides of this field, passing a church and three footpath markers and stiles going off to the right, and leave the field in the far corner.

Join an unsurfaced track and turn left. This is an unclassified county lane.

After 500 metres turn right through a metal kissing gate and enter an arable field. Walk ahead with a wire and post fence and hedgerow to your left.

Follow the trodden path around to pass through a metal kissing gate into a second field where there's a small stream under the hedgerow to your left. Cows are possible in this field.

Cross the stream at the wooden footbridge and turn right, with the stream now to your right.

Stay in this direction, passing under telegraph wires.

At the end of the field go through a metal gate.

Cross the farm lane to enter a field and continue ahead with the stream and a hedge over on the right.

Aim to the right of a farm house ahead, pass through a usually open farm gate and continue forward to join a country lane.

Turn right onto the lane and head upwards, passing Keeper's Cottage on your left.

Just before the lane bends right, turn left through a gate to the side of a cattle grid.

Walk on an unsurfaced track to the side of first a young plantation and then the mature trees of Alne Wood.

Pass 'Mutton Barn' to the left and stay on the bridleway into a further plantation of young trees.

Pass under telegraph wires and immediately turn right, and then left to follow a woodland track.

This brings you to an open gateway and field where you continue in the same direction to the far side of the field.

Here you'll see a yellow topped waymarker post. Turn right, ignoring a mass of footpath arrows all pointing to the left. Your path is the unmarked Arden Way.

Keep the hedgerow and a deep dew-pond to your left and at the end of the field pass through a nearly invisible metal gate hidden in the hedge.

Walk across the next field towards farm buildings and exit onto a farm way.

Bear right, past the modern barns, and continue to a T-junction with a little used country lane and turn right.

Just after Glebe Farm turn left and pass through a gap to the right of a metal gate and walk with the hedge on the right. You're now crossing to the side of a racehorse training area, so dogs on leads here.

Pass storage sheds on the left and continue with a wooden fence to the left.

Enter the next field and keep the hedge on the left.

Pass under telegraph wires and go through a metal gate on the left, and then bear right. Follow this path forward until you reach a private tarmac lane. Do take care to keep dogs on the footpath and out of the horse paddocks.

Turn left on the lane, going uphill, and then turn right just before Hill Farm.

Go through a metal gate, with footpath markers, and walk through a set of small paddocks and turn right after the last enclosure and before the silage heap ahead, and through a metal gate. The path isn't immediately obvious here.

Head downhill, and through a further metal gate and into woodland.

Keep descending through the trees, using the occasional footpath marker as a guide. The path is much neglected, and common sense is the best guide to a safe route down the slope here.

Continue through the woods to emerge onto a country lane and turn left.

You're now just outside the hamlet of Maudslay. Turn right onto a track before the first house on the right (Whitts End). This is the other end of the track from the start of the walk.

At the 'unclassified road' sign and yellow waymarker, turn left into the field, and retrace your route past the church and through a field to return to Great Alne.

Walk 13
Aston Cantlow

Refreshments: The Kings Head, Aston Cantlow, Warks, B95 6HY
Tel: 01789 488242 Opening hours and menus: www.thekh.co.uk

Shakespeare's parents, Mary Arden and John Shakespeare, were married in Aston Cantlow church and then enjoyed a wedding breakfast at the Kings Head. Certainly this lovely pub is old enough to have hosted a 16th century wedding party, so history is all around you. Today the surroundings are rural chic with a sophisticated menu to match.

Dogs welcome in the bar and in the garden seating area.

Walk map

Walk info

It could be said that Aston Cantlow lies in the heart of Shakespeare Country, with many connections to properties owned by members of the Arden family. Mary Arden's house is in the nearby village of Wilmcote, and the young William Shakespeare would have been brought to visit his grand-parents here.

Length: 5 miles (8km)
Stiles: 8 (one awkward stile for large dogs if adjacent gate is locked)
Livestock: sheep possible in 2 or 3 fields
Suggested OS map: Explorer 205 Stratford-upon-Avon & Evesham
Parking: The King's Head car park, B95 6HY with permission
Nearest vet: Severn Veterinary Centre, 20A High Street, Henley-in-Arden, B95 5AG. Tel: 01564 792444
Waste bins: by church; Maudsley

Start Point: The King's Head car park OS map: SP138598

Walk 13 Route

Leave the Kings Head car park, enter the churchyard through the lychgate and immediately take the left waymarked path (Arden Way). Cross over the footbridge, this has a stile with dog-gate on the far side, and into a field.

Go straight across the field towards Aston Grove, the wooded hill ahead, and climb another stile.

Cross over the lane, bear right and join a farm track a few yards further on the left.

Walk on the farm track until it bends to the right. At this point leave the track and carry straight on into a field to walk with a hedge to your right.

Keep heading towards Aston Grove, and cross over a stile at the end of the field.

Turn left on the lane and after 100 paces or so turn right and through a gate with a footpath waymarker.

Continue towards the woodland and enter the woods through a metal gate close to the fence on the left.

Walk on the woodland path around the fringe of the woods and turn right at a footpath marker leading to a kissing gate on the right.

Walk down the side of a field with a hedge on your right. Then turn right through the open gateway at the end of the field and then immediately left, clearly marked with waymarker posts. Walk through this field and the following two fields with the hedge to your left.

Emerge from the fields onto a farm track and turn right. Join the country road and turn left. This is Walcote, a tranquil Warwickshire village of medieval origin.

Pass Walcote Manor Farm and walk through the village to the Old Vicarage.

Detour: opposite the Old Vicarage is a path to Haselor church. It's just a few minutes out of your way, and worth a visit. There's a particularly charming book of villagers' embroidery samples and a wall hanging. Views from the church are delightful on a fine day.

Take the footpath on the right immediately after the old vicarage and walk down the field with the vicarage garden on your right. Pass through the gateway, or over the adjacent stile, and carry on into a field with a hedge to the right.

Climb a double stile/footbridge combo into the next field – dogs can go round to the right of the stile under a wire fence or, if slim, there's a dog gap to the left. After rain this can be muddy.

Continue in the same direction in the next field, keeping your dog to heel as you approach the trees because of a lane ahead. Pass through a kissing gate and down the steps in the bank and onto a country lane. Listen for vehicles here, there isn't much room for tractors and walkers.

Turn left and then almost immediately right to cross a narrow footbridge over the River Alne.

Stay in the same direction over the flood meadow ahead, and then bear left and past a tennis court.

Ahead is the former Great Alne mill, now converted to private homes, but retaining its two splendid air chimneys.

Follow a series of footpath arrows to walk past the mill and over the Italianate wooden footbridge, and pass through the residences to a lane.
Turn left onto the lane, and after 20m go through a metal kissing gate on the left and into a field.

Head diagonally right towards the middle of the hedge and pass through a kissing gate into the next field.
Bear half-right, aiming for the middle of the long side of the field, and across the faint traces of an old railway line into the next field.

Bear diagonally left and over a step-stile – there's plenty of space for dogs to go under the fence railings – and head downwards to the left corner of the field.

Go through a rickety wooden gate to emerge onto the busy Alcester Road and turn right.

Cross over the road with care and turn left at the wooden sign for the church (dog waste bin here).

Walk up to the church and turn right to walk behind it and through a wooden gate. Enter the field and go straight on towards a stables clock. The path is enclosed by hedges on both sides as you approach a lane in the hamlet of Maudslay (dog waste bin).

Cross the road and take the signed footpath up a few steps ahead and walk on the fenced-in path. Go left when the path forks, and pass a village cricket ground to your right.

At the end of this path (dogs on leads) turn left onto the Alcester Road and after 250 metres turn right onto an unsurfaced track. Take great care here as the turn is on a corner and on-coming traffic can't see you.

Pass an electric sub-station and turn left down through the trees. The footpath markers are hard to spot, if you reach a ford you've gone too far.

After a disused railway bridge, go over a stile and turn left to cross the field (sheep possible here) and pass over a double stile and footbridge.

Follow the narrow path with the river to the right and emerge at a caravan park (dogs on leads) and stay clear of the geese.

Stay on the tarmac drive to leave the park and cross the river again to reach a lane. Take an immediate left onto a signed footpath by a dog waste bin. This brings you back to the church in Aston Cantlow, and the King's Head.

Walk 14
Wootton Wawen and Knowles Wood

Refreshments: The Cowshed, Yew Tree Farm craft centre, Pettiford Lane, Wootton Wawen B95 6BY. Tel: 01564 792979. Opening hours and menus: http://yew-tree-farm.co.uk/fine-food-drink

Hidden in a corner of the Yew Tree Farm craft centre is The Cowshed; a licenced eatery where you'll find home-made meals, cream teas and cakes. There's a warm, almost farmhouse kitchen feel to it and tables by the wood-burner are rarely empty for long in winter. A very inviting place indeed.

Dogs are welcome inside, and at the garden tables outside.

Walk map

Walk info

The village of Wootton Wawen dates back to Saxon times and was one of the most prosperous and powerful settlements in the area for many years. The imposing church of St Peter now houses the Saxon Sanctuary Exhibition, which tells the fascinating story of the village. Entrance is free and it's well worth a visit after your walk.

Length: 6 miles (9.5km)
Stiles: 0
Livestock: sheep likely after Cutler's Farm
Suggested OS map: Explorer 220 Birmingham
Parking: Yew Tree craft centre walkers' car park. Pettiford Lane, Wootton Wawen B95 6BY
WCs: next to Cowshed café
Nearest vet: Avonvale Veterinary Centre, 5 The Rosebird Centre, Shipston Road, Stratford-upon-Avon, CV37 8LU Tel: 01789 561010
Waste bins: several on canal towpath

Start point: Yew Trees craft centre OS map: SP158631

Walk 14 Route

From the craft centre, cross the road and head up the lane marked 'Private Road to Lucy Farm'.

At the canal bridge (dog waste bin) turn left onto the Stratford-upon-Avon canal towpath. Continue as far as bridge 51.

Turn right to cross the canal at bridge 51 and follow a track between the hedgerows. This is on the route of the Monarch's Way.

Enjoy the path as it makes its way through Austy Wood. In spring the floor is carpeted with bluebells. Continue to the top of the hill, then follow the Monarch's Way arrow to the left at a fork in the path.

The path leaves the wood and bears right into a field.

Head downhill, pass through a gap in the hedge, and continue down to go past the barns of Cutler's Farm to your left and outbuildings now converted to a small business centre.

Turn right on the hard-surfaced track.

Pass by one footpath marker on the left.

After 450m bear left across the grass after the second oak tree and cross a footbridge with kissing gate to enter a large field.

Turn left in the field and then turn right at a footpath marker to walk gently uphill, and close to a few trees marking an earlier field boundary on your left.

Turn right at the top and carry on to the far side of the field where you then turn left into the next field, walking with the hedge on your right.

Turn right on the well-trodden path through a gap in the hedge and after a few paces turn left to join a holloway between the fields (Monarch's Way). Holloways are often the remains of old trackways, left in place after fields were enclosed and often used by landowners to ride around their farms and see who was working hard and who was slacking.

Turn left when you reach a clearing, this is at the end of the second field on your left and you'll see a yellow-topped waymarker post.

Walk up the field with the hedgerow to your right, and then follow the path through a kissing gate. Now head on a diagonal line to a gate in the far right corner of this field.

Turn right onto an access track.

Continue to a crossroads of path and lanes and turn left. Pass through a kissing gate to the left of a farm gate onto a shaded track, through a further gate and keep straight ahead on the track.

Follow this into Knowles Wood (approx. 400m). After a further 60m or so bear left when signed with a footpath arrow.

The woodland path through Knowle's Wood has been thoroughly signed with direction arrows at every twist and turn of the route. Follow these to a final gradual descent, and you'll emerge in a field.

Turn right and continue, following the field's hedge line. You'll quickly reach the Cutler's Farm access lane, where you turn right.

Turn left after the farm-house, cross the farmyard and up the slope ahead to retrace your steps from the start of the walk.

Bear right at the top, turn left to enter the woodland at the footpath marker and continue downhill on the Monarch's Way through Austy Wood.

Turn left at the canal bridge (51) to join the towpath, and at bridge 53 turn right to return to the craft centre.

Notes

Walk 15
Henley-in-Arden

Refreshments: The Nag's Head, 161 High Street, Henley-in-Arden B95 5BA Tel: 01564 793120 Opening hours and menus: https://www.facebook.com/pages/The-Nags-Head-Henley-in-Arden

Recently renovated and under new management the Nag's Head is one of the most dog-friendly pubs in the historic market town of Henley-in-Arden. The building itself is seriously old, and a warm and welcoming atmosphere has built up over the centuries.

Food is reasonably priced traditional pub food and the local sausage and mash option is generous, and filling.

Dogs are welcome in the bar and at the outside tables in the large garden behind the pub.

Walk map

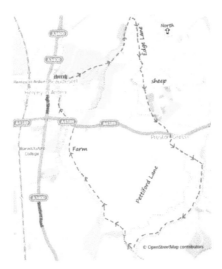

Walk info

Henley-in-Arden is a small town with many fine timbered black-and-white houses along its High Street. A small Heritage Centre tells the story of the town, and how many medieval customs survive to the present day through the Court Leet. The oldest feature in the town is the hill at the start of this walk, once the site of a 12th century motte and bailey castle.

Length: 5 miles (8km)
Stiles: 0
Livestock: cows likely in one field; sheep likely in two fields
Suggested OS map: Explorer 220 Birmingham
Parking: The Nag's Head car park (£-with refund for pub customers) or Prince Harry Road (free) car park (B95 5GD)
Nearest Vet: Severn Veterinary Centre, 20A High Street, Henley-in-Arden (corner of Rose Avenue), B95 5AG Tel: 01564 792444
Waste bins: at start point; on canal towpath

Start point: St Nicholas church, corner of Church Lane and Alne Close OS map: SP153659

Walk 15 Route

Go through a metal kissing gate on the corner of Church Lane and Alne Close.

Pass a dog waste bin to the left and head up the small hill ahead. This is the site of a motte and bailey castle, built in the 12th century by Thurstan de Montfort. You'll see traces of the earthworks as you walk over the site, but little else. Descend by the steps on the far side, and continue in this direction up the slope ahead.

Pass a wooden bench, handily placed to admire the view if you're out of puff, and carry straight on ignoring two signed footpaths and stiles on the right.

Step over the wooden fence, dogs go through a large gap to the left, and turn right.

You'll soon reach a wooden gate onto an earth track; this is the original Edge Lane – once a busy thoroughfare for riders and country-folk on foot.

Turn right and follow the track, which eventually becomes surfaced, to walk past Kyte Green Farmhouse. Dogs on leads here.

Turn left on the lane ahead and then turn right onto a footpath beside a 5-bar gate just around the corner.

Follow the driveway to a further walkers' gate to the right hand side of outbuildings and keep going on the narrow path to the far side of the property.

Go through the kissing gate ahead and stay in the same direction past a barn and then go straight across two fields. Sheep are likely here

There's a stile at the far side, next to a farm gate which does open if you or your dog find stiles difficult. Pass a house on the right (dogs on leads here, there's a road ahead) and bear right to walk up to the busy Warwick Road.

Cross with care onto Pettiford Lane.

Turn left immediately after the 'triangle' on Pettiford Lane and take the footpath signed at a wide grassy verge.

Walk downhill on the footpath and stay in the same direction to cross the field ahead. If there's been recent ploughing, aim at the wooded knoll on the skyline to stay on the footpath line.

Cross a footbridge and turn right onto the towpath of the Stratford Canal.

Stay on the towpath for 1.6 km (1 mile) as far as Bridge 51 (dog waste bin here).

Take the bridleway on the right (or take the lane/driveway at the earlier bridge 50 in very wet weather).

Continue as far as Pettiford Lane, turn right, walk on the road across the bridge and then take the first footpath on the left at a farm gate.

Cross the field diagonally to the far right corner and follow the path over two more fields, staying close to a stream on your left.

Enter the third field and turn right, away from the stream and with a hedge to your right. Follow the hedge to bend around the corner of this part of the field.

The path then goes straight towards a farmhouse (Blackford Mill Farm).

Skirt around Blackford Mill Farm on the signed route to the right of the building, past the barns on the far side and into a final field - expect cows here. Keep the blackthorn hedge to the left and emerge onto the busy Warwick Road at the far side. Cross the road and bear left as far as Prince Harry Road where you turn right.

Keeping the stream to the right, leave the pavement and continue alongside the stream onto the grass. The stream makes an excellent paw-wash for muddy dogs just before you cut through the car park to an archway leading to the High Street. Turn right to reach the Nag's Head.

Notes

Walk 16
Preston Fields

Refreshments: The Crabmill, Warwick Road, Preston Bagot, Warks, B95 5EE. Tel: 01926 843342 Opening hours and menus: www.lovelypubs.co.uk/venues/the-crabmill

An outside view of The Crabmill takes you straight into the 17th century, when the building was used to press crab apples to produce cider. Inside, you'll find a modern rustic and friendly atmosphere where diners mingle sociably with walkers, and well-behaved dogs.

Dogs are welcome in the bar and at the garden tables. Dog biscuits are served to deserving canine visitors.

Walk map

Walk info

A shorter walk, ideal for a stroll before or after enjoying a visit to The Crabmill.

Length: 3 miles (5 km)
Stiles: 6 (4 easy for dogs, and 2 with dog gates)
Livestock: cows/sheep possible in two fields
Suggested OS map: Explorer 220 Birmingham
Parking: The Crabmill car park, with permission. B95 5EE
Nearest Vet: Severn Veterinary Centre, 20A High Street, Henley-in-Arden (corner of Rose Avenue), B95 5AG Tel: 01564 792444
Waste bins: on canal towpath

Start point: The Crabmill OS map: SP171653

Walk 16 Route

From The Crabmill car park turn left onto the Warwick Road. Walk with care to the second left turn (no through road) and pass Preston Manor.

Go through a wooden gate by Lock 38 onto the Stratford canal towpath and turn right, walking with the water to your left.

Walk as far as the next bridge, 45. Don't cross the bridge, but bear right and down a few steps into a field.

Turn left and walk parallel to the canal for the length of the field.

Bear a little to the left and go over a stile in a small copse and into a second field.

Pass through a gate-sized break in the hedgerow and into a further field, still with the canal on your left.

Just before the end of this field, turn left to go over a stile onto a canal bridge.

Cross the canal and towpath and continue straight ahead on a footpath. It's hard to spot, but definitely there.

Reach a metal gate and go through into a field. Follow the path diagonally across the field and then go through a metal kissing gate.

You'll see a small brook on your right, and your path stays to the left of this brook over the next two fields. On a hot day, dogs will be glad of a drink or a splash in the cool running water.

When you reach a metal kissing gate, cross the lane and continue straight ahead and through another kissing gate into the field ahead.

With the brook still to your right, continue across the next two fields to a pair of low stiles and footbridge.

Carry on across a further field in the same direction, and note that there is a high probability of sheep in the field on the other side of the brook and the fencing is non-existent in places.

At the end of the field there's another stile, and this one has a lift-up dog gate to the side. Go over the stile and cross the next field to reach a further stile with dog-flap.

Turn left after the stile onto Preston Field Lane, an unclassified lane used by cyclists, walkers and horse-riders and enjoy the shade for 750m.

The final section is surfaced, and becomes an access lane to the few houses here. Continue past the houses (dogs on leads) and then turn right onto a quiet country lane.

Walk as far as a finger post sign to Preston Bagot church, and just after this turn left through a metal kissing gate into an arable field. Follow the trodden path downhill.

Turn right after the hedgerow on the right. Now walk with the hedgerow to the right to the end of the field.

Turn left, still in the field, and then turn right to cross a footbridge over the river. Water-loving dogs will discover several small 'beaches' ideal for swimming here, but do watch the current after heavy rain.

Take the right-hand fork in the path and this leads you back to the canal towpath at Bridge 46. Cross the bridge and walk along the towpath with the water on your right. Leave the canal at the wooden gate by lock 38, and turn right on the road to return to The Crabmill.

Walk 17
Preston Bagot and Tattle Bank

A second walk from The Crabmill, simply because their food is so lovely!

Refreshments: The Crabmill, Warwick Road, Preston Bagot, Warks, B95 5EE Tel: 01926 843342. Opening hours and menus: www.lovelypubs.co.uk/venues/the-crabmill

Walk info

The hamlet of Preston Bagot was recorded in the Domesday Book, making it an older settlement than nearby Henley-in-Arden. Today it remains a very rural area, with scattered farmhouses and an agricultural focus.

An Art Barn, housed in the Old Rectory, holds regular art and sculpture exhibitions and is within walking distance of The Crabmill

Length: 5 miles (8km)
Stiles: 1
Livestock: cows or sheep likely in one field; chickens around a farm
Suggested OS map: Explorer 220 Birmingham
Parking: The Crabmill car park (with permission if not taking refreshment)
Nearest Vet: Severn Veterinary Centre, 20A High Street, Henley-in-Arden (corner of Rose Avenue), B95 5AG Tel: 01564 792444
Waste bins: at entry to canal towpath

Start point: The Crabmill OS map: SP171653

Walk map

© OpenStreetMap contributors

Walk 17 Route

Leave the Crabmill and turn left onto the Warwick Road. Cross the River Alne and a motor lane, and then turn left at a No Through Road sign. Immediately after crossing the canal bridge, turn right to join the Stratford Canal and then cross under the Warwick Road on the towpath.

Follow the towpath across a bridge to reach the other side of the canal (dog waste bin here) and continue, walking with the water on your left.

At the next bridge, number 49, cross over the canal.

Turn right to go over the stile. A dog detour through a nearby metal farm gate to the left is possible if this low stile proves difficult.

Cross the field diagonally and go through the gate at the far corner.

Aim for the telegraph post in the centre of this next large field. Then you'll be able to see a gate directly ahead. Livestock are often in this field.

Go through the gate at the end of the field and onto a grassy track. Dogs on leads here, chickens and other farm animals are likely.

Follow the yellow footpath arrows around the paddocks and pigsties near the farm buildings and then turn right onto Kington Lane after the kissing gate.

Around the corner, pass a lovely old barn and then turn right at the signed Private Road/Bridleway just after Kington Grange.

The track leads to Chestnut Stables, where you bear left to stay on the bridleway.

The bridleway is well signed with blue markers, and is very easy to follow.

Continue on the track through fields, beside a wire stock fence. Sheep usually graze on the other side.

Pass some cottages on the right, and outbuildings of Cutler's Farm – now converted to office units. Don't be confused by the number of footpath signs leading in every possible direction. Keep going past the outbuildings and then turn right before the farm house, and walk with the courtyard office units and barns on the right.

There's a clearly trodden uphill path in the field after the barns, it swings right around the edge of the trees at the top of the slope.

Look out for a gate on the left, and go through this into Austy wood.

Stay on the bridleway through the trees, ignoring one footpath going off to the left. Continue gently downhill until you reach a canal bridge.

Cross the canal bridge and turn right to walk on the towpath.

Leave the towpath at bridge 47 and return to the Crabmill.

Notes

Walk 18
Lowsonford

Refreshments: The Fleur de Lys, Lowsonford, Warwickshire B95 5HJ Tel: 01564 782431 Opening hours and menus: www.fleurdelys-lowsonford.com

Whether it's a freezing cold day or a baking afternoon in summer, the Fleur de Lys is one of those welcoming country inns where you just feel you're in the right place at the right time. The inn became famous in the 1950's for its fabulous home-made pies, served on newspaper from a hatch by the kitchen range. Pies are still served here, but now on a plate and with cutlery!

Dogs are welcome in the large garden and in the bar – the restaurant is a dog-free zone.

Walk map

Walk info

Lowsonford's a pretty Warwickshire village with strong connections to water. The name originates from 'lonesome ford', and the canal came to the village in the late eighteenth century. A railway used to run through the village, but this stopped when its tracks were taken up and shipped to France to be used in the trenches during World War 1. The tracks never made it to France as the transport boat was sunk in the Channel.

Length: 4 miles (6.4km)
Stiles: 2
Livestock: unlikely
Suggested OS map: Explorer 220 Birmingham
Parking: Fleur de Lys car park
Nearest vet: Avonvale Veterinary Centre, 5 The Rosebird Centre, Shipston Road, Stratford-upon-Avon, CV37 8LU Tel: 01789 561010
Waste bins: on the canal towpath

Start: Fleur de Lys, Lowsonford OS map: SP187679

Walk 18 Route

Leave the Fleur de Lys car park and turn left onto Lapworth Lane. Cross over the canal bridge and then turn right to walk into a small Waterways car park (dog waste bin here) to the Stratford canal towpath.

Turn right and pass under bridge 41, walking with the water on your left. Continue to the next bridge (number 40) past the garden of the Fleur de Lys.

Leave the canal at the bridge (dog waste bin), turn right on a lane to cross the canal and walk up to a crossroads.

Turn right, past the old village water pump and continue on the lane through the village.

Shortly after passing the sides of an old railway bridge turn left onto a lawned grassy patch and through a metal gate onto a public footpath.

Follow this path ahead to a kissing gate, and then around to the left.

At the metal gates ahead turn right, walk up the slope to the woodland ahead on the Heart of England Way.

Go over a wooden stile (large gap for dogs to the right) and into the woods, following the path downhill. You'll emerge into a small field.

Turn right, and you'll reach a three-post livestock and cyclist deterrent.

Turn right after this and join a bridleway leading gently upwards.

Stay on the bridleway for around 1km, past The Field House and Keepers' Cottage. At the end of the track turn left onto Bushwood Lane.

Walk for 250m and when the lane bends to the right, take the footpath up a bank on the left.

Walk with the woodland (Bush Wood) to your left across five fields, going over one stile (with plenty of space for dogs to pass through) and finally through a metal farm gate.

In the 4th field you'll spot some dilapidated sheds tucked in amongst the trees. At one time this was a scene of huge excitement for point-to-point meetings, and it's easy to imagine bets being placed through the 'shed' windows.

Aim to the right of the farmhouse ahead, and emerge at a metal gate in front of the house. Dogs should be on-lead through the farm buildings.

Turn right, pass a couple of bungalows and then turn left into a field through a metal gate at a footpath marker. Cross the field on a wide trodden path, bearing slightly left to go through the farm gate ahead. Turn immediately right after the gate.

Continue to a signed path into the woodland on your left. You should recognise the route now, as it retraces your steps back to the Fleur de Lys. Leave the woods, go over the stile and down the sloping field to the metal gates at the bottom. Turn left and follow the path to reach Lowsonford village. Turn right at the lane and continue straight ahead to the Fleur de Lys.

Walk 19
Lowsonford and Yarningale

Refreshments: The Fleur de Lys, Lowsonford, Warwickshire B95 5HJ Tel: 01564 782431 Opening hours and menus: www.fleurdelys-lowsonford.com

The Fleur de Lys is blessed with a spacious and comfortable canal-side garden, where a 'swift half' can effortlessly extend to a much longer stay. It's so easy to sit and watch the canal boats passing by! On cooler days you'll find a lovely warm traditional interior, with blazing fires and a number of delightful seating sections.

The food is freshly prepared, with a tempting specials board.

Dogs are welcome in several of the bar areas, and outside in the garden.

Walk map

Walk info

A second walk from Lowsonford, this time exploring a different part of the surrounding countryside.

Length: 4 miles (6.4km)
Stiles: 1
Livestock: cows possible in one field
Suggested OS map: Explorer 220 Birmingham
Parking: Fleur de Lys
Nearest vet: Avonvale Veterinary Centre, 5 The Rosebird Centre, Shipston Road, Stratford-upon-Avon, CV37 8LU Tel: 01789 561010
Waste bins: waterways car park, and canal towpath

Start: Fleur de Lys, Lowsonford OS map: SP187679

Walk 19 Route

Turn left on the lane from the Fleur de Lys and follow it round to the left (signed Shrewley). Go over the canal bridge, don't miss the Antony Gormley sculpture on the left, and turn left onto a track directly opposite the waterways car park.

After a few paces turn left to go through a metal gate by the yellow topped waymarker and carry on with the brook on your left and a fence on your right. Notice below and on the left the characteristic shape of one of the idiosyncratic barrel cottages, unique to the Stratford Canal.

The path heads gently up a slope and bends round to the right. At the top of the incline, bear slightly left with the path with the fence on your right.

Go through a metal kissing gate and keep to the left in the grassy field. At the corner of the field, turn right to continue in the same field with a hedgerow on the left. Pass to the right of a wooden outbuilding, ignore a gateway on the left, and continue with the hedgerow on your left to go through a metal kissing gate. Although it seems strange to walk around three sides of a field, that's where the path lies.

Continue gently downhill on a controlled
path with a hedge on your left and
paddocks on your right. Cross over the
gallops with care and keep straight on
with the paddocks on your right and
through a metal gate.

Head for the far left corner of the field
with a red brick house directly ahead.
Cross over a footbridge and then follow
the path around to the left to go over
another small bridge, then turn
immediately right to walk with a wooden
fence on your left and past some farm
buildings. Follow this path, through two
metal gates, and emerge onto a lane.

Turn left on the lane and, before
reaching a house on the left, turn right
onto a track.

Follow the track around to the left. Go
past two cattle grids, then through a gate
to the left of a third. When the track
bends right to lead to a farmhouse, carry
straight on through two farm gates to
enter a pasture field. Carry straight on in
this field, keeping the hedge on your left.

At the bottom of the field, go through the metal gate and bear diagonally across the field to the far right corner. Keep going as the field funnels, and you'll reach a small fresh-water stream.

You will see three metal gates. Take the kissing gate to the left (with a yellow footpath arrow) and walk across the field with the stream on your right.

Go through a metal kissing gate, across a ditch and over a stile and carry straight on in the next field. There is a wire and post fence on your right as well as the stream.

After 200m turn right to cross over a footbridge and into a field.

Continue up the gentle slope and keep going straight, the trees start to come closer in, and at the end of the field go through a metal farm gate.

Bear right to cross a small field and go through the two metal farm gates on the far side to reach a lane. Turn right on the lane and keep on the left hand side of the grassy triangle.

As the lane bears round to the left, turn right down a bridleway (No Through Road sign). There is also a small sign saying "To the Field House".

At the Field House, turn left along the track (do not go through the wooden gate with footpath sign ahead). You are now walking along an Unclassified County Road. Keep on this track, ignoring any footpath signs to left or right. This road is shared by a small stream at wet times of the year.

Keep on the unclassified road as it bends round to the right and continue straight on, passing Valley Farm on your right.

Continue straight, passing through two wooden posts. Pass Hobbs Hole Cottage, where the footpath returns to unclassified road status.

 Pass a further house on the right.

 When the unclassified road meets a lane, turn right and walk to the end, passing several charming residences.

 Take the well-signed footpath to the right side of 'The Cottage'. Go up a few steps and the Stratford Canal is ahead of you. Turn left and immediately cross over the canal at Bridge 44a, opposite a barrel cottage.

 Turn right onto the towpath, walking with the water and the tiny, but fascinating Yarningale Aquaduct on the right.

Continue as far as Bridge 41 where you leave the canal and return to the Fleur de Lys.

Walk 20
Rowington to Baddesley Clinton

Refreshments: Tom o'the Wood Country Inn, Finwood Road, Rowington, Warwickshire CV35 7DH. Tel: 01564 782252 Opening hours and menus: www.tomothewood.co.uk

Popular with walkers and cyclists, the Tom is always a welcome sight at the end of a walk. The menu doesn't disappoint, and dogs are always assured of a plentiful supply of biscuits. Dogs are welcome in the bar and conservatory, and at the outside tables.

The curious pub name comes from a 17th century windmill, probably used for grinding corn. The high ground of Rowington was a good place for catching the wind, and other historic windmills in the area had the names of Bouncing Bess and Pinchem.

Walk map

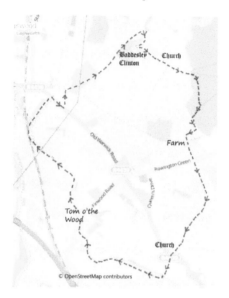

Walk info

This walk passes by the moated 13th century manor house of Baddesley Clinton, now a National Trust property, and also close to Shakespeare Hall in Rowington. It is said that Shakespeare worked on the play 'As You Like It' whilst staying with relations at Shakespeare Hall.

Walk length: 5 miles (8km)
Stiles: 2
Livestock: Sheep likely in two fields, cows probable in two fields
Suggested OS map: Explorer 220 Birmingham, and Explorer 221 Coventry & Warwick
Parking: Tom o' the Wood car park (with permission).
Nearest vet: Avonvale Veterinary Centre, 43 Birches Lane, Kenilworth CV8 2AB Tel: 01926 854181
Waste bins: on canal towpath

Start point: Tom o' the Wood OS map: SP193697

Walk 20 Route

Turn left from the car park and walk on the lane to cross over the canal bridge, and immediately turn left to reach the Grand Union canal towpath.

Turn left, to walk under Bridge 63 towards Kingswood Junction with the canal to your right.

Pass under Bridge 64.

Continue on the towpath, and cross the footbridge (67) to keep walking alongside the Grand Union, signed Birmingham by a lovely old fingerpost on the opposite bank.

At Bridge 65 leave the canal and ascend to a road. Dogs on leads here, it's a fast country road and there is no pavement when you emerge. Cross the road with care and turn right, passing the Navigation Inn.

After 50 meters turn left onto a cinder driveway, opposite The Manor House. A footpath arrow (Heart of England Way) marks the way, but you may have trouble seeing it amongst the surrounding weeds.

Go through the gate and pass a house on the right and then follow the track round to the right, with an equestrian barn to your left.

Now follow the signed footpath through a series of paddocks. Dogs on leads if they can't manage a perfect 'heel' here.

Go through a kissing gate at the end of the paddocks, enter National Trust land, and go straight on over the next field. A hedge will be on your right. Sheep are possible here.

Ignore a National Trust footpath signed to the right and carry straight on over a stream and through a kissing gate into another field.

Keep the hedgerow to your right and when this ends, bear half-right (45 degrees) aiming for a wooden gate ahead. Sheep are likely here.

Look to the right for a fine view of Baddesley Clinton house. (National Trust)

Go through the wooden gate and turn right onto the Baddesley Clinton access lane. Walk down to the entrance to the hall and then turn left, signed to St Michael Church.

NT members can enjoy a detour into Baddesley Clinton, where you'll also find a café and WCs. Only assistance dogs are allowed in.

Pass through the churchyard and onto a broad track. At the gate at the end (dogs on leads) cross the country lane and carry straight on and into Hay Wood.

Turn right onto a forest path as soon as you enter the wood, ignoring the footpath posts and arrows you may notice on the left. Hay Wood is marvellous for dogs, with lots of enticing scents and plenty of shade from the trees. You'll emerge onto a forestry track after 10 minutes walking or so.

Turn right on the track and walk down to the vehicle barrier. Turn left here (dogs on leads) and walk on the lane as far as the first gate on the right, about 50 meters.

Turn right onto the track to Green Farm and walk towards the farm house past a barn and byre to the left. Keep dogs on leads here, not just because of the farm vehicles and livestock but also because the grounds are policed by an enormous tom cat with a murderous attitude to dogs of all sizes.

Walk through the farmyard, past the picture-book perfect traditional farmhouse and pond and to their gate.

Cross the lane and go straight on through a kissing gate by a yellow footpath marker and into a field. Go straight across the field and notice the converted windmill 'Bouncing Bess' on the right.

Pass through a kissing gate and go straight on in the next field, towards a clump of trees.

Bear slightly right, keeping the hedge to your right, through a metal gate and up a gentle slope. Pass through a kissing gate at the top and continue straight ahead, signed with a marker arrow.

Follow the path down a small slope and through an open gateway. Cows are likely here. Continue up a small slope to reach a stile in the left corner of the field.

Walk past the Old Rectory, to go over a rather awkward stile leading to the churchyard of St Laurence, Rowington.

If the church door is open, a visit inside to see the authentic painted ceiling is worthwhile.

Leave by the church lych gate and cross the lane with care, you're right on a corner here. Bear left on the pavement and down a hard surfaced bridleway.

Cross over a canal bridge and immediately turn left to reach the towpath. This is again the Grand Union canal.

Turn left on the towpath and walk underneath the bridge (62).

Leave the canal at bridge 63 and cross the bridge on the lane to return to the Tom o' the Wood.

Notes

Walk 21
In the Tapster Valley

Refreshments: Tom o' the Wood Country Inn, Finwood Road, Rowington, Warwickshire CV35 7DH. Tel: 01564 782252 Opening hours and menus: www.tomothewood.co.uk

Walk map

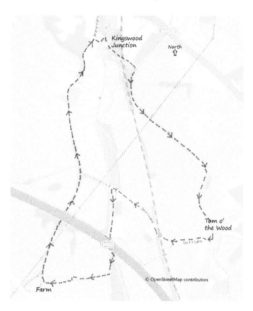

Walk info

This walk could be called 'transport through the centuries', as the route takes in old roads, now green lanes, two different canals, under the mainline railway and over a motorway too.

Walk length: 3.5 miles (5.5km)
Stiles: 0
Livestock: very unlikely
Suggested OS map: Explorer 220 Birmingham
Parking: Tom o the Wood car park, with permission
Nearest vet: Avonvale Veterinary Centre, 43 Birches Lane, Kenilworth CV8 2AB Tel: 01926 854181
Waste bins: on canal towpaths

Start point: The Tom o'the Wood OS Map: SP193697

Walk 21 Route

Leave the car park and turn left on the lane. Go over the canal bridge and shortly afterwards turn right, Dick's Lane. This is a no through road that gives access to two houses – dogs can be off lead.

Pass under a railway bridge and reach the second house – a barrel cottage unique to the Stratford canal. This one has been much extended but you can still see the original barrel, formed by using the mold of the lock inverted to create a house for the lock-keeper.

Turn left on the canal towpath and continue, passing under the M40, to Lock 27 'Lapworth Bottom Lock'. Immediately after this cross a narrow footbridge at Bridge 39b. Turn left, leaving the canal, and through a metal gate to enter a field.

Turn left in the field and walk as far as the next footpath post. Turn right to walk straight across the field. At the far side of the field turn left.

Turn right at the next yellow-top waymarker through a metal kissing gate that's almost concealed by a hedge, and walk along the side of the next field with the hedge on your right.

Bear right at the next yellow waymarker, over a plank bridge, and through a metal kissing gate to emerge onto a farm track. 'High Chimneys' farm buildings will be to the left.

Turn right and continue on the track. This soon narrows and becomes a 'green lane'. Stay on the green lane, ignoring all footpath signs to the left and right, and pass underneath the motorway again.

When the path splits, take the left fork marked with the blue arrow of a bridleway and not the unclassified county road.

Continue straight and past farm buildings, still on the bridleway which is now a wider track sometimes used by farm vehicles.

When the track meets a tarmac road (Brome Hall Lane) turn right after Foreman's Cottage and go through a wooden gate on the left and pass to the left of 'The Mill'.

This is Kingswood Junction – where the Stratford and Grand Union canals meet. Take a few minutes to explore the Junction – there's plenty to see.

Turn right over Bridge 36 and cross the Stratford Arm, then follow the 'arm' to join the Grand Union, and follow the towpath round to the right signed towards Warwick.

Walk on the towpath as far as Bridge 63 and you'll see the Tom o' the Wood again.

Walk 22
Tanworth-in-Arden

Refreshments: The Bell Inn, The Green, Tanworth in Arden, Solihull B94 5AL Tel: 01564 742212 Opening hours and menus: www.thebellattanworthinarden.co.uk

The Bell takes pride of place in the centre of this much photographed village and, as well as serving appetising meals, also provides the local community with its post office and village shop.

Dogs are welcome in the bar area and at the outside tables on the charming village green.

Walk map

Walk info

Tanworth has claim to two famous sons, both creative talents who died tragically young. Bruce Chatwin the novelist, and the musician Nick Drake. The village has deep farming roots, and this walk shows off the soft Warwickshire countryside of oak trees and gentle slopes at its best.

Length: 4 miles (6.4km)
Stiles: 3
Livestock: cows likely in one field, sheep likely in another field
Suggested OS map: Explorer 220 Birmingham
Parking: The Bell Inn car park with permission, or on street in the village
Nearest Vet: Severn Veterinary Centre, 20A High Street, Henley-in-Arden (corner of Rose Avenue), B95 5AG Tel: 01564 792444
Waste bin: near Tanworth village green

Start point: In front of the Bell Inn OS Map: SP113705

Walk 22 Route

Turn left out of the Bell car park, cross the road and turn right through the wooden gate into the churchyard and carry on around the church, keeping it to your right. The churchyard attracts fans of the late Nick Drake, the musician, who lived in the village and is buried here.

At the path crossroads, turn left. Continue along the path to leave the churchyard through a kissing gate and into a field. The countryside opens up here with views across fields and low hills.

Keep to the left hand side of the field and go through a metal kissing gate set in the hedge and down some steps onto Butts Lane.

In medieval times longbow practice was compulsory, and archers were expected to fire an arrow over 400 yards into a 'butt', or mound of turf with a target on top. It's very likely that Butts Lane was used for archery practice, with the targets placed where the red brick farmhouse 'The Butts' is now.

Turn right on the lane and walk for about 20m, then turn left onto a footpath. This can be muddy in wet weather.

Keep straight on with the hedge on your right and soon you'll be walking with the remains of an old orchard on your left.

Go over a plank bridge and stile (plenty of room for dogs to the side) and enter a field.

Keep to the right in this field with the hedge on your right and, when the field bottlenecks, cross over the wooden bridge.

Now cross the narrow field ahead, through a gate and under the railway line. Follow the track over a stile into the next field.

Bear right in this field and continue to its end. If you look behind, you will see a white house and farm buildings. These are part of Umberslade Farm Park. The railway line is to your right, electricity cables carry on down the middle of the field, and there is a stream which follows the line of the trees to the left. The railway is well fenced off.

The field narrows down like an arrowhead. At its end, cross the stream over the footbridge and stile.

Carry straight on in the next field, and two yellow topped posts can be seen to the right. Ignore the first one (with its metal kissing gate and footbridge) and take the direction of the second post to go through a metal kissing gate, keeping the stream on your right.

Continue alongside the stream in the cultivated field.

Go through a gate on the right into a further field. Keep on the flat here, don't go up the slope.

Go through another metal kissing gate and keep straight on along the left side of the new field. The slope is to your left, the stream to the right.

After 100m go through the double metal kissing gate into another field (sheep likely). Keep to the right hand side of this and all subsequent fields until you reach a farm track leading up to Bickers Court Farm.

Turn right on this track, passing a bungalow on your left and up to a country lane, with the rustic name of Pig Trot Lane.

Turn right onto the lane and continue up to a T-junction, passing a house called Lockerbie on the left. Turn right at the T-junction onto Danzey Green Lane, signed Tanworth.

After 40m turn left onto the farm track for Meadow Farm. The track goes over the railway line and continues straight on, passing the farmhouse on the left.

Very soon, you arrive at a choice of three gates. Go through the middle gate, faintly signed as a bridleway, and continue into the field (livestock likely). Keep to the right hand side. Mockley Wood can be seen over on the left.

At the far end of the field, go through a metal gate into a new, cultivated, field. Keep to the left hand side, following the barbed wire fence as it bends gently around to the right. Another farm appears ahead. The barbed wire fence then becomes a hedge.

145

Go through the gate and follow the track towards this farm (Forde Hall), keeping the hedge on your left.

Follow the path as it makes its way around some farm buildings and emerges onto a lane.

Turn left onto the lane and after 20m turn right to enter the farmyard. Pass the farmhouse on your left, then bear right and immediately left past the cowsheds.

Continue past a slurrystore on the left and go straight on into a new field. Keep to the right hand side (by a wire fence), following the line of the electricity cables on your right.

At the end of the field, climb over the stile and wooden footbridge next to the left hand metal gate. The path now runs alongside a copse.

At a fork in the path opposite a red brick house (Little Ford Hall), turn right to cross a plank bridge and through a metal gate. The path is badly overgrown here, and easy to miss.

The path now runs alongside the driveway to Little Ford Hall, passing through some gates, and leading gently uphill. Near the top of the hill you should be able to see the spire of Tanworth Church.

At the end of the track turn left, passing Grange Hall on your left. Follow the hard surfaced lane around to the right, then keep straight on through a gate.

Turn right and walk past two barns on the right. Immediately after the second one, go through a metal gate on the right to a footpath and cross a track into the field beyond. Walk down the left hand side of the field, parallel to the farm driveway.

At the end of the field, go through the kissing gate and plank bridge, cross the lane and straight on through another kissing gate into the final field. Aim for the far left corner. Leave the field through a kissing gate and turn right on the road. Stay on this road passing Far Leys, once the home of the Drake family, and then turn right at the T-junction to return to The Bell.

Notes

Walk 23
Lapworth to Copt Green

Refreshments: The Boot Inn, Old Warwick Road, Lapworth, Warwickshire B94 6JU Tel: 01564 782464
Opening hours and menus: www.lovelypubs.co.uk/venues/the-boot-in-lapworth

The Boot is a friendly and welcoming inn, with a large garden for summer and a traditional flagstone bar with a warming log fire for the winter. You'll find tasty food and a lovely relaxed atmosphere.

Dogs are welcome in the bar, and at the outside tables.

Walk map

Walk info

The canal system at Kingswood Junction is a highlight of the walk, and it gives a fascinating insight to the history of our canal systems.

Length: 5 miles (8km)
Stiles: 2
Livestock: possible in one field
Suggested OS map: Explorer 220 Birmingham
Parking: At The Boot, walkers' car park
Nearest vet: 608 Vet Practice, 608 Warwick Road, Solihull, B91 1AA. Tel: 0121 705 3044
Waste bins: several on canal towpaths

Start Point: Entrance to the canal OS map SP180711

Walk 23 Route

Leave the walkers' car park and turn through a wooden gate to join the Stratford canal towpath.

Turn right to pass under some overhead pipes, walking with the water on your left. The towpath here is quite close to the road so dogs under close control here. Go underneath a small bridge with care as there is no separation between towpath and road.

At lock 19 you'll find yourself at the canal junction where the Stratford Canal meets the Grand Union Canal.

There's lots to look at here at Kingswood Junction including useful interpretation boards, a marina, and lots of little bridges.

Cross over bridge 36, pass lock 20 and a typical Stratford Canal barrel cottage on your right. Go over another bridge (36a) then immediately turn left, signed Grand Union.

Go under the railway bridge (36b) and turn right at bridge 37 (don't cross it) and continue down the towpath with the canal on your left. This is now the Grand Union Canal. Be aware that the railway line is nearby on your right and can be reached by dogs if not under control.

Pass under bridge 64. Leave the canal at bridge 63 and turn left onto the road.

Take the first turning to the right, Dick's Lane, and walk down the lane to the end, passing under the railway to a barrel house.

Go straight across the canal bridge and follow the path through the hedgerow.

At the path T-junction, turn left.

Keep straight on to pass under the M40. Follow the farm lane as far as the unclassified county road, then follow the black arrow to the right (following the line of the electricity pylons). You will see farm buildings to the left, and shortly after you reach a lane. Turn left here.

Opposite Grange Cottage, turn right through a gate into the field (if you pass a lane to the right, signed Henley, you've gone a little too far).

Walk in the field with the hedge to your left and go through a large gap on the left and into a new field.

Keep going in the same direction with the hedge now to the right. Pass under electricity wires and then bear right (yellow waymarker) down a sunken path between the fields.

Emerge into a further field and walk with the hedge on the right to a gap at the far side and pass through this onto a lane. Turn right on the lane and immediately go round a corner. Pass over a couple of small bridges which cross a fresh-water brook.

Turn right at a yellow footpath marker at the next farm gate. Go diagonally across the field aiming for a telegraph post in the far corner, to the left of a small red brick cottage.

Go through the gap in the hedge to meet a country lane and turn right. You are now in the hamlet of Copt Green. Pass Yew Tree Cottage and the gateway for Keeper's Cottage. Pass a metal kissing gate and footpath sign on the right and then take the footpath on the left shortly afterwards, marked with a yellow waymarker post and metal gate.

Bear half-right after the gate and go underneath the cables aiming towards the oak trees ahead. You should be able to see the spire of Lapworth church slightly over on your right.

Go over the wooden stile ahead (space for dogs on left) and turn right, walking at the edge of the field with the hedge to your right.

Just before the end of the field, turn right at a yellow waymarker post and go through the hedge and over a plank footbridge with kissing gate into the next field and walk along two sides of the field, passing a cottage on the way, to the far corner.

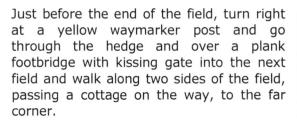

Leave the field through a kissing gate. Cross over the brook (there is a stile at the start with a dog hole on the right). There's fresh water at the brook for dogs to drink and dip their paws in.

Cross the lane and follow a track straight ahead.

Cross over the motorway (well fenced, but dogs on leads is recommended).

Shortly after a double farm gate, turn right to cross a footbridge and go through a metal kissing gate and into a field. Ignoring the stile straight ahead, turn left to walk round the outside of the field.

Walk past the house ahead, staying on the wide enclosed path. This will lead to a footbridge and kissing gate.

Go through to emerge into a field and follow the line of oak trees to your right. Then bear off to the right, aiming for a visible kissing gate in the cricket pitch fence. There may be livestock in this field.

Go into the cricket ground of Lapworth Cricket Club (dogs on leads here) and keep left. Leave through the small car park gate and the Stratford canal will be ahead.

Turn right on the canal towpath at bridge 30, walking with the water to your left at first and then on the right before the Lapworth Flight of locks. There are dog waste bins aplenty on this stretch of the canal.

Keep following the Stratford Canal as far as Lock 14, then turn right before the overhead pipe to return to The Boot.

Notes

Walk 24
Lapworth and Hay Wood

Refreshments: The Navigation Inn, Old Warwick Road, Lapworth, B94 6NA. Tel: 01564 783337
Menu details and opening hours:
http://www.navigationlapworth.co.uk

The Navigation lies on the Grand Union canal and was originally a popular watering-hole for thirsty bargees. These days there's more fun to be had watching novice holiday-makers on the canal from the large waterside garden.

The menu offers traditional country pub meals with a modern twist, and thirsty walkers may appreciate the rare chance of Guinness on handpull.

Dogs are welcome in the main bar and in the large canal-side garden.

Walk map

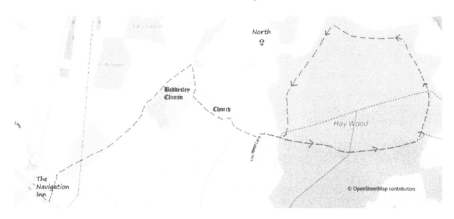

Walk info

Shakespeare is said to have written 'As You Like It' whilst staying with relations in nearby Shakespeare Hall and it's a popular local belief that he strode around Hay Wood to get the creative juices flowing. Today, the woodland is managed by the Forestry Commission and the trees are young conifers.

Length: 5 miles (8km)
Stiles: 0
Livestock: possible in one field
Suggested OS map: Explorer 220 Birmingham
Parking: The Navigation car park
Nearest vet: 608 Vet Practice, 608 Warwick Road, Solihull, B91 1AA. Tel: 0121 705 3044
Waste bin: Baddesley Clinton car park

Start point: The Navigation OS map: SP190709

Walk 24 Route

Leave The Navigation car park and turn left on the road. After 200m turn left onto an unsurfaced track.

Pass through a kissing gate and bear right around an equestrian barn.

Walk on a grassy track between horse paddocks to a gate on the far side to enter National Trust land.

Go straight ahead in the next three fields, keeping the hedge on your right.

You may be able to spot the manor house of Baddesley Clinton through the trees on the right. It's a delightful 13th century moated manor house, now maintained by the National Trust.

Pass through a gate and walk half-right ahead, with Baddesley Clinton over to the right, and through the next wooden gate.

Turn right on the access lane and walk past the National Trust car park towards the visitor centre.

Turn left on an unsurfaced track to the left of the entrance to Baddesley Clinton.

Reach the church and pass it to the left. Continue through the churchyard to a track on the far side.

Walk to the end and cross the lane to continue on the grassy track directly opposite.

Enter Hay Wood and turn left on the forest path.

When you reach a waymarker post turn right, signed with a blue bridleway arrow.

Cross a wide track and go straight on to the far side of the wood, signed with a blue arrow.

Turn left, and continue to walk anti-clockwise around the outside of the wood. There are no arrows to follow, but the forest path is fairly clear.

In most places you should be able to see fields beyond the trees on your right side.

After 40 minutes or so, you'll see the waymarker post from the start of the walk again on your left.

Retrace your footsteps by turning right down the grassy track to return to the church and Baddesley Clinton.

Take the wooden gate on the left after the car park and follow the footpath across the fields to return to The Navigation.

Respect the countryside

Many of the walks in this book go through farmland. Please respect the farmers who work hard to grow crops and raise livestock by:

Staying on the footpath through fields

Walking in single file through crops

Not allowing your dog, or children, to trample crops

Picking up after your dog

Walking calmly near livestock

Avoiding getting close to, or between, cows with calves

Keeping your dog on a lead – but if you feel threatened, let the dog go and get yourself to safety

Being aware that herd animals are territorial – always spot safe places to leave a field should you need to

Reporting injured farm animals to the nearest house, if possible

Dogs in pubs

At the time of writing, all the pubs used in this book are dog-friendly in the bar areas and gardens, not in the restaurant sections. This privilege may be withdrawn at any time if other customers are upset by just one dog's poor behaviour. So please make sure your dog is well-behaved, and is never allowed on seats, to eat off plates or annoy other customers in any way.

About the Author

Lezli Rees lives in Warwickshire and is a keen walker and rambler. A firm believer that regular exercise is important for people and dogs alike, she organises the Explore by Paw Warwickshire dog walking group and runs the popular Driving with Dogs website.

Lightning Source UK Ltd.
Milton Keynes UK
UKHW020402101120
373078UK00008B/376

9 780992 719739